God's GOT YOUR Back

God's GOT YOUR Back

IT'S IN HIS WILL

WANDA EASON

Pleasant Word

A Division of WINEPRESS PUBLISHING

ISBN 1-57921-686-2
Library of Congress Catalog Card Number:
2003106413

Dedication

This book is dedicated to my Grandmother, the late Missionary Ora Mae Johnson and Mother, Deaconess Daisy Jackson, for their guidance and grace that taught me to be a real woman of God. I would also like to dedicate this book to my sons DeAndre and Brandon, my family and my dear cousin Sonya Johnson who I love so dearly and who wasn't afraid to believe God with me. Last, I would like to dedicate this book to a dear friend, Sharon, for all her support and to the late Suzonne "Sue" Goodley for giving me positive support and friendship . . .

Table of Contents

Acknowledgment 9
Introduction 11

Chapter 1: Called By God 13
Chapter 2: It's in His Will / In the Will of God ... 21
Chapter 3: No Weapon Shall Prosper,
    I Am in Battle 25
Chapter 4: Marriage 31
Chapter 5: Spiritual Growth 45
Chapter 6: The End of the Chapter/
    The Beginning of a New 49
Chapter 7: Devil, I Identified You! 53
Chapter 8: Church Affairs 61
Chapter 9: Where Do I Go from Here? 67
Chapter 10: Peace That Passeth All
    Understanding 69
Chapter 11: Waiting on Him 75

Chapter 12: Paying a High Price 81
Chapter 13: If God Says "Go" 87
Chapter 14: The Word Brought Me through 91
Chapter 15: Conclusion: Know Your Choice..... 95

Special Thanks 101

Acknowledgment

First to my Lord and Savior Jesus Christ, who is the author and finisher of my faith, I would like to thank my mother, Daisy T. Jackson who has been so instrumental in helping me to the next level in God. To my brother Angelo and Melissa Pettis who has been a tower of strength in times of need. To my sister Coletta Hill, thanks for being a true friend. Missionary Emily Hill, Missionary Mattie Tucker and Missionary Gloria Wright, for their encouraging words and Spiritual Guidance. Prophetess Holmes for helping me to fight in the battle. Mr. Rufus Jackson for telling me never to give up. Willie Johnson for being a great grandfather.

A special thanks goes to my pastor, Bishop H. D. Bryan, Sr. and his loving, sweet wife, Mother Almarie Bryan, and to the entire Holy Redeemer Church of God in Christ family, Ft. Lauderdale, Florida, for their prayers and support.

Introduction

I must tell my story!

While reading the Word of God one night the Lord interrupted my studies and began to speak to me about His Will in my life.

He allowed me to think back into past and present experiences of my life that forced me to acknowledge His awesome powers of protection. The Lord began to show me how each experience was a piece of a puzzle that would complete His purpose in my life.

It was clear that "Satan" desired to destroy me in every situation. But the Lord spoke to me saying "Wanda, I am going to use each trial to make you into the Woman of God I want you to be. My perfect Will in your life will be *done*."

In the midst of an overwhelming trial in my life, the Lord said, "I want you to tell your testimony." I replied, "Lord, who am I, but just a plain Christian?" and again He said, "Tell the story and I'll open the door." At that moment, 1:00 in the morning, I sat on the floor with pen in hand and started to write. The Lord gave me the revelation to help someone who needs to know His power as a protector. My life is a testimony that Jesus Christ can keep you in presence of danger, seen and unseen, in your life.

When reading this book, open your heart and mind to be encouraged. No matter what the devil has planned in your life or what you've been through, God will protect you. "God's Got Your Back!"

CHAPTER 1

Called By God

When I was a little girl, growing up in a small town in Georgia, going to church had always been apart of my life. My grandmother, Missionary Ora Mae Johnson, would attend faithfully and made sure the family knew whom God was and what He could do if we trusted Him. I would listen to her and I began to watch her life. I realized God was a good God.

By the age of thirteen, I was helping out at the church and assisting in the Sunday School Class. One Sunday morning, the late Pastor McGriff of East Park Church of God, said that they needed a Sunday school teacher and I was the one. I couldn't believe what I was hearing. Little me was going to teach the adult Sunday school class. Well I did.

Years went on, one night during a revival while sitting the church, the enemy (Satan) attacked my legs, and it felt as though I was never going to walk again. My grandmother and Bishop Husband of Church of God in Christ, laid hands on my legs and rebuked the enemy and loosed my legs. At that time the church mothers and the Pastor looked over me and said, "This girl has a calling on her life."

At the age 11, I could not process this experience that set my life into motion. It was the power of the spoken Word of God. Pastor McGriff and Bishop Husband laid hands on my head and spoke the Word that God's Will would be done in my life.

As years went on I was attending the church, but the church was not in me. It was not until 15 years later, 1986, when I moved to Fort Lauderdale, Florida. I received the Holy Ghost and the Word that was in me would start to manifest itself in my life.

As I grew older, my life would start to change. I continued to serve the Lord through my high school days. My friend gave me the nickname "The Pope," and would always come to me for prayer. At this time I knew I was saved. I attended college and moved back home. In the same year, at the age of

21, I got married (a virgin) and life couldn't be better. Little did I know this was about to be a process that would determine my place in God.

I never believed that I was a minister for Christ. All I wanted was to be saved and that was all. I never wanted anything else. However that wasn't what God had in mind for my life. The Lord began to use me to speak during different services at the church and He moved in a powerful way. This was not all that was going to happen in my life.

A door was opened in October 1997 during a youth revival. I was four months pregnant with my third child. That night I wasn't scheduled to preach but they asked me to bring the Word of God. The topic was "God's Got Your Back!" I had preached like I never did before.

The next day I attended school, being a teacher by profession. After getting off from work, around 2:30 P.M., I went home. I put one foot in the house and my water broke. At first I stood there for a few minutes. My body was stiff, I couldn't believe what had just happened. I knew then that this was trouble. I panicked and started to cry. Within a minute, everything that I had preached to so many people the night before began to ring in my mind.

At first I couldn't pray. All I could do was look down at the water on the floor. I ran to the phone and called the doctor. I then called my mother, but she worked twenty minutes away and that was too far. So I called my Godmother, Minister Emily Hill, who was an anointed Women of God. She came to my house, picked me up and we went to the doctor. In my mind, I started to question God, but something happened that day. The Lord was holding me up. About seven days went by and the doctor kept me in the hospital. The saints came by in big numbers, I felt "God used them to minister to me."

At this time, I delivered a son and had to go through the delivery; that resulted in a miscarriage.

Each time someone came by, all I could hear was "God's Got Your Back." After the trial, the Spirit of the Lord used me even more. I began to depend completely on God's Word (Psalm 34:19). I told myself daily, "I would bless the Lord at all times."

In this trial I was able to tell men and women that God was a healer, a mind regulator, and a strong tower. The devil meant for me to lose my mind, but God gave me the victory.

In this situation I would often tell myself, "I am going to find a way to praise God." The Bible tells us that the "joy of the Lord is our strength." Every chance I got; I praised God with everything that was in me. The more I praised God the better I felt.

Thou wilt not deliver him unto the will of his enemies. (Psalm 41:3)

He will give *strength* to his people. This was just another step in my process to God.

Months went by and the Lord allowed me to preach again in a state conference. In the midst of this, the devil continued to come against me. The day I found out I had to preach, everything broke loose. I just purchased a brand new 1999 Toyota Avalon. The dealer called me that day and said "We are sorry but you've got to bring the car back." I could not believe this, here I had told people how God had blessed me and now the devil was about to steal my joy. Look here, through this trial, watch God's power and protection be fulfilled. Before it was over I drove away with a new 1999 car for 5,000 dollars less than what the dealer had offered at the beginning. After I preached that night, the spirit spoke to me while I was riding home in the car, "You're not in it alone." God let me know at that very moment that "I'll be with you always and never forsake you." *Romans 8:28* says "It's all for My good."

And we know that all things work together for good to them that love God, to them who are the called according to His purpose.

We praised the Lord for the moving of His Power. The Lord is in charge of our lives. He will direct our every move, if we trust Him.

Before every elevation in God, there has to be a trial of your faith. I didn't understand that until now. Unless you understand the move of God in your life you will not understand what it means to suffer with Him in your trial. In the midst of your trial, the Lord will lead and guide you into all understanding. If we want to be something in God and have His Holy Spirit in the anointing, we must prepare for the battles that are going to come.

Many are the afflictions of the righteousness; but the Lord delivereth him out of them all. (Psalms 34:19)

The Lord will deliver His people out of every battle that is against you. So no matter what you're going through, God's Word has a way out.

After this trial I said to myself "I know this has to be the last trial, for right now." The enemy jumped into my finances and my home. My home was in foreclosure and I had to prepare myself to vacate the premises. I knew then that God had to step in and work a miracle. Through prayer and belief in His Word I knew He would not allow myself and my children to be out on the street. This situation again proved to me that "God Had My Back." He fixed it where the house at this stage was savable. The Word of God states in *Proverbs 3:5–6* that we need to trust God like never before and He would make everything right.

> *Trust in the Lord with all thine heart; and lean not unto thine own understanding. In all ways acknowledge him, and he shall direct thy paths.*

With each situation, I felt God moving me up to another level.

CHAPTER 2

It's in His Will / In the Will of God

What is God's Will in my life? That was the question I asked myself over and over again. The Word of God states in *Philippians 2:13* that:

> For it is God which worketh in you both to will and to do of his good pleasure.

Jesus on one occasion stated "Not my will Lord, but that Your Will would be done in my life." In order to know His purpose for your life you have to be in His Will.

> I can of mine own self do nothing: as I hear, I judge: and my judgment is just; because I seek not mine own will, but the will of the Father which hath sent me. (St. John 5:30)

Jesus was letting His disciples know that His Father in heaven was His witness to what His purpose for coming to this world was going to be. In order to receive God's Will in your life, you must prepare for it to happen. We must find ourselves seeking Him daily, always asking Him, "Lord, what will you want me to do this day?" Nothing in this world can stop the Will of God in your life. It does not matter what the enemy has put in your way, you can have whatever God has for you if you're in His Will.

When the Lord was speaking to David in Psalms 34:19, I don't think people of God really hold on to the power of this verse, "but the Lord delivereth him out of them all." When David had to flee from Abimeleeh, he completely allowed God to be his protection when he found himself in God's Will. You can't do anything without God as the head. Because sooner or later whatever you are doing will fall apart.

Some of you may argue the fact and say "I trust God, I am in His Will and I still have troubles in my life." Troubles and trials in your life don't mean you are not in His Will. Several times I had to tell myself that, because it seemed as though the devil was winning in the battle. The Lord spoke and revealed to me that the strategy of Satan is to cast doubt in your mind about God's Will in your life. Satan's sole purpose is to deceive, steal, kill, and to destroy the people of God. So when he comes with these thoughts and ideas, you must find yourself praising and lifting up God even more. Remember, however it looks, "God Will Prevail!"

At this time in your life, don't give up. Don't throw in the towel; hold on a little while longer. Help is on the way. God has a fresh Word for His people. When you're in His Will, the enemy can't mock God. Everything God has promised He is well able to perform.

> *Let us hold fast the profession of our faith without wavering for He is faithful that promised.* (Hebrews 10:23)

One thing you can count on is what God says, stand on His Word.

> *The Lord is not slack concerning His promise as some men count slackness; but is long suffering to us ward, not willing that any should perish, but that all should come to repentance.* (2 Peter 3:9)

When God has a purpose for your life, He takes full responsibility for any action that Satan is allowed to put on you. When God says enough is enough then Satan has to leave you alone. Let's notice the suffering of Job. The Word says Job was a perfect and upright man of God, But Satan was allowed to touch Job's surroundings. Job did not let go of God. He stated on one occasion, "The Lord giveth and He taketh away." This let the enemy know that no matter what he did, Job had sold out to God.

As Christians, we must stay in His perfect Will in order for God to work on our behalf.

CHAPTER 3

No Weapon Shall Prosper, I Am in Battle

God has a purpose for your life. The devil comes but to steal, kill, and destroy.

Notice in *Ephesians 6:10–13*:

> *Finally, my brethren, be strong in the Lord, and in the power of his might.*
>
> *Put on the whole Armour of God that ye may be able to stand against the wiles of the devil.*
>
> *For we wrestle not against flesh and blood, but against principalities, against powers, against the rulers of the darkness of this world, against spiritual wickedness in high places.*

*Wherever take unto you the whole Armour of God
that ye may be able to withstand in the evil day,
and having done all, to stand.*

In order to fight, you have to be in position. As Christians we need to prepare for the battle. The key to winning is you have to keep your mind. Don't let the enemy take your mind. The Bible states we are transformed by the renewing of our mind.

If I have my mind together, the devil can't run my life. Because the Spirit of God is controlling my life, I know I have the victory. *1 Corinthians 15:57* reads:

*Thanks be to God which giveth us the victory
through our Lord Jesus Christ.*

Paul was letting us know that we already are a winner. No matter what battle you are in, the Lord will never lose.

When you apply the Words "No weapon formed against me shall prosper" than you know that you have the victory through God. This is a powerful scripture. Everything that the enemy has plotted against my life, family, children, job or my finances, won't work. The Lord has always made a way of escape for His people. If you can control your mind by having every thought in captivity, accepting the good ones and rejecting those from the devil (2 Corinthians 10:5*) then you have a weapon to fight the enemy with.

> *Casting down imaginations, and every high thing that exalteth itself against the knowledge of God, and bringing into captivity every thought to the obedience of Christ.*

As Christian warriors by using the Word of God you can put the devil on notice that God's Word has more power than anything else. It's through the blood of Jesus that you are sanctified, made holy, and set apart for God's use! We must become armed and dangerous for the Lord. Satan does not scare easily. When Paul had preached in Ephesus, he showed a powerful move of God. However when the seven sons of Sceva a Jew; a chief priest tried to cast out an evil spirit without the Holy Ghosts power, the evil spirits said, "Jesus I know, and Paul I know, but who are ye?" The demons knew the power of God and they also knew who really has the anointing in their life needed to cast demons out of a person life. As a warrior, you must be willing to be sold out to God. Willing to take a stand in the evil world. It's no time to be playing church. You have to be for real. As a believer in Jesus Christ, we have authority over any ruler of darkness. It's not your self's will but through the Spirit. So God Don't Need Any Coward Soldiers! I preached a message once, "Killing It At The Root." Anything in your life not like God, get rid of it. When we resist the devil in our lives, the enemy must flee. The enemy does not fight fair, he hits below the belt all the time. Scripture to study: Psalms 35:1–3 and Psalm 37:1–4. In all things we should "Commit thy ways unto the Lord, trust also in him and he shall bring it to pass."

Everything in your life that is not going right, trust in the Lord and he will bring it to pass. Someone once said to me "Two things that God and the devil have in common is they both want to use you! But it's up to you who you want to be used by." Our thought should be. Use me Lord and speak to my heart. Let your Holy Spirit abide. In God our battles are already given the victory. No matter what I am going through I will not speak defeat. I'll say to myself—I have:

VICTORY OVER DEFEAT

LIFE OVER DEATH

PEACE OVER WAR

JOY OVER SADNESS

In the midst of the struggle you must find a way to praise God. By keeping your mind on the Lord, He will direct your every move. It will come a time in your life when only God can lead you out or through a situation. There is always a war going on in your mind. Therefore protect your mind. He will keep you in perfect peace, whose mind is stayed on Him.

You might say Sister Wanda, what does this have to do with battle. Everything, because if you have a bad mind, you can't fight the enemy.

CHAPTER 4

Marriage

God ordains marriage. The Lord desires for His people to live happily in a relationship that He joins together.

> *"So God created man in his own image, in the image of God created he him; male and female created he them."* (Genesis 1:27)

The Lord went on to tell us how close a male and female really are *Genesis 2:21–24.*

> *And the Lord God caused a deep sleep to fall upon Adam, and he slept: and he took one of his ribs, and closed up the flesh instead thereof:*

And the rib, which the Lord God had taken from man, made he a woman, and brought her unto the man.

And Adam said, This is now bone of my bones, and flesh of my flesh: she shall be called Woman, because she was taken out of Man.

Therefore shall a man leave his father and his mother, and shall cleave unto his wife: and they shall be one flesh.

In these scripture it describes how a man shall leave his father and mother to cleave unto his wife. This means that nothing should come between this union.

The act of marriage is that of a beautiful and intimate relationship shared uniquely by a husband and wife in the privacy of their love—and it is sacred. In a real sense, God designed them for that relationship. Proof that it is a sacred experience appears in God's first Commandment to man: "Be fruitful and multiply, and replenish the earth (Genesis 1:28).

And God blessed them, and God said unto them, be fruitful and multiply, and replenish the earth, and subdue it: and have dominion over the fish of the sea, and over the fowl of the air, and over every living thing that moveth upon the earth.

That charge was given before sin entered the world: there lovemaking and procreation were ordained and enjoyed while man continued in his original state of intercourse. Therefore marriage deals with each person on a social relationship, but our relationship with God is spiritual. God, the Holy Spirit is silent on the subject either, for He endorsed this sacred experience on many occasions in scripture. In *Hebrews 13:4* he inspired his writer to record this principle:

> "*Marriage is honorable in all, and the bed undefiled . . .*"

Nothing could be clearer than this statement. God's word is right to the point. Because the Bible clearly and repeatedly speaks out against the misuse of abuse of sex, labeling it "adultery" or "fornication." God condemns these things. Therefore if you marry someone then having a sexual relationship with the person you marry would be correct. I know now you might be saying, yes that's right. Wrong! God must choose the person in order for the marriage to work.

> *I BESEECH you therefore, brethren, by the mercies of God, that ye present your bodies a living sacrifice, holy, acceptable unto God, which is your reasonable service.* (Romans 12:1)

Based on what God has done, you must present your body a living sacrifice. God does not ask us to do anything until He does something first. If you want to have a relationship, you must have your self together in order for the relationship to work. Self is the base for any relationship. You can't have a relationship without you being involved. The part that you can have the most control of any relationship is yourself. But first you must be able to get along with your self. As Christians, we must have a relationship with God. God does not want man to be alone. God knows man's mental state, He looked into man's mind and decided he should not let man be alone. God knows our relationship with Him is spiritual, but man also has social needs. God does not provide the social part, because God's relationship with man is spiritual. Some needs God won't meet, but He will provide.

> *Prayer will keep you but it cannot satisfy the social side of man. Prayer connects to God—through the glory of love. Our fight is to stay in line with God, no matter what the circumstance may be.*

The Bible states that it is not good for man to be alone. However it does not mean that you could not live alone. Morally it could not be wrong because Jesus and Paul were alone.

Sometimes you can prosper by your self. It's not desirable to be alone. As humans we want to have someone to talk to, in order to fulfill the side. God would rather you be alone, but if you must, first pray and fast, not later.

When you are alone, the enemy deals with your mind, making you feel inferior. Satan will provide somebody to use you, because you are willing to give up God to not be alone. Instead, focus on being unique and you should refuse to let anything in your life that does not please God.

When you find out that a relationship is not pleasing God, it can and will destroy you. God knows how to solve our problems. When God allows Satan to enter in any relationships, He takes complete responsibility, and He knows when to make the devil leave you alone. When God is in a relationship "No weapon formed against a relationship can prosper." As Christians we must realize that God is the giver of life and He knows what we need and when we need it. If you override the spirit of God, get ready for a mess. God knows how to bless a relationship.

Therefore you must wait on the leading of the Spirit. God is a jealous God, there shouldn't be anything or person that you put before Him. We have a spiritual and fleshly side of our lives. The spiritual side often tells you not to get involved, but the fleshly side controls your mind.

> And the Lord God said, It is not good that the man should be alone; I will make him a help meet for him. (Genesis 2:18)

In order to be lead by the Spirit, you must allow the Spirit of God to have complete control. Adam was split between his relationship with God and the woman God gave him. Adam allowed Eve to make him disobey God. Adam put his relationship with God in jeopardy. Do you choose to please God? When you choose to please self then you may not please God.

As Christians, we must praise God for allowing us to have a relationship because if it's not God's will, then a marriage or relationship will not last. The problem comes when we select someone that does not please God, trouble will be all around. Adam jeopardized his relationship with God by choosing something outside of God's plan. When God directs your choice, in a relationship there is going to be a way already made. Sure there are going to be problems but God will help keep it together. Don't leave God to make your own choices, because the devil will give you something that will destroy your life. Allow God to help you find a mate.

When God is not in control, get ready to go through some changes. You will never be able to please your partner. If your choice is not of God, you have to keep adjusting to keep up with the other person. Some days they love you, some days they don't. It does not matter how someone else feels, you are trying to adjust to someone else's feelings in order for you to feel good about yourself. You spend too much time trying to control someone else's feelings toward you. God does not want your mind so out of control. The Bible states "He will keep you in perfect peace who's mind is stayed on Him." You cannot find peace in God in a relationship that is not formed by God.

Pain and suffering is not of God. When you find that someone is happy when you are hurting that is not of God, nor is it His will in your life. When helping to keep a relationship is hurting you, this does not please God. Because in hurting yourself, you cannot give yourself over to God's will. In a relationship that is not of God, neither person could be happy. The Lord must qualify you and allow you to see that you are beautiful, special, and unique. In order for someone to love you, you must first love yourself. You can't let your emotions cause you to choose your heart. The mind and the heart are in different places. Don't allow your heart to control your mind.

In making changes, your mind must be in charge. You must be transformed by the renewing of your mind when choosing a mate. If not, you'll find yourself attracted to people who are of the flesh. These people are not the mate that God intends for you. Many times we stay in a relationship because of the flesh. We say that we just "clicked" or the time was right. Really what is happening is your flesh controls your spirit. When you have the same unclean nature and spirit, you attract your own kind. This is how you end up with someone who is not good for you. However, when you go through the process of purification, you will see that this is not the right person. This difference can take place at any time in a relationship that is not of God. When two people join together, they will become one flesh when God is first.

When I got married, I wasn't thinking about any of this. I must admit I didn't pray about the relationship. I allowed how the person looked spiritually on the outside to determine my choice. In entering a marriage, you promise to be together "until death do you part." This was and still is my belief. No one told me to minister to the man. I was too young and immature to understand that praying first, before getting married would help in the relationship.

Looking back, I should have prayed more about God's choice of a mate for me. It's a major decision, so please take your time.

> *Be careful for nothing; but in every thing by prayer and supplication with thanksgiving let your requests be made known unto God.* (Philippians 4:6)

If your mate does not come through prayer and supplication, your relationship has an unstable foundation. If you date or marry in the flesh, trouble and problems will already be brought into the marriage. This is my story. Because of my lack of the knowledge of God's Word, there were conflicts in my marriage before I said "I do." I had no idea that missing this step would cause me to suffer and go through hell on earth for the next several years of my life.

Many times marriages are never solid from the beginning. During the first few years, things may begin to happen that will concern you early on. On the outside everything looks perfect. We believed that Christian marriages are supposed to be a match made in heaven, but was God pleased with your choice? As couples, you should go through counseling. The announcement of the engagement was made and I waited for the wedding day.

After the engagement, I went back to college to finish my degree in school. All that was on my mind was getting married and how I had kept myself all these years. The question I should have been asking was, "if God was ready for me to make this choice in my life?" This was the biggest mistake you can ever make.

Trust in the Lord with all thine heart; and lean not unto thine own understanding.

In all thy ways acknowledge him, and he shall direct thy paths. (Proverbs 3:5–6)

You must always ask God for direction especially in selecting a mate.

Months went by and I continued to plan the wedding with the help of my mother and family members. This was one of the most special days of my life. But did I consult God? The ceremony was beautiful. I had over fifty people in the wedding party. Everybody seemed so happy for us. However, there was one major problem that continued to hang in the balance. . . . Did I ask God for an answer about my choice?

Before the wedding a lot of unforeseen problems took place. Lost wedding bands, the bridesmaid's dresses were taken, and the caterer backed out at the last minute. However, the wedding still went on.

The wedding was wonderful and we consummated the marriage. Things couldn't be better. Marriage vows are powerful. The joining of two people becomes a stronghold in the spiritual realm. But when you enter into a marriage, with someone who is not the Will of God for your life, you have to be prepared for the consequences. My consequence was nothing small and very painful. For years, I lost my identity as a person. I became someone I didn't like and didn't want to be.

A marriage can become one of control and complete domination. We often give complete control of our life to our spouse. In doing this I left my first love. The way a person feels about you becomes more important than the way God sees you.

When I married I was a virgin, being naïve can blind you of many things in a marriage. After being

married for many years, you have children and believe that this will bring you closer.

However, on the outside it can look like a happy
family; but on the inside you can feel a lot of pain
and grief.

In a marriage you may start to argue about fi-
nancial problems, day care and many more household issues. This can cause an earthquake in your
marriage. Many times your spouse can make you
feel as though you're not making them happy. Yet
around other people you seem to be having it going
on. It can get to the point where negative statements
can be made that can crush and break your heart.
This can become a small hill or a great mountain in
your life. Each year you will begin to see less of your
strength and more of defeat.

In a marriage you see changes that should be
stopped early on. The pattern can be right in your
face but you refuse to see it. Because of the denial,
the enemy takes over your family and your marriage.

At church we tend to wear our masks; however,
at home we become a different person. We find ourselves losing the identity of a person, causing un-
happiness through conversation and sexually. Have

you ever invested time in a relationship, to having being told, "Your not my partner!" After receiving the answer to these questions, should you leave while you are ahead? However, we want to be married. If change is not made, this can go on and on, until your life is no longer on track. We find ourselves giving so much to someone else and not enough to God.

We also find ourselves, not praising God like we should. When your mate is not happy with you, you are not happy with yourself. It was not until you find out that there is more going on in the marriage than you could see. The Lord however, can bless you to preach His Word and in doing so, He gives you strength to deal with the changes that takes place in your life. It was as though He said, "Ready or not here it comes."

CHAPTER 5

Spiritual Growth

Spiritual Growth is never easy. God never said that it would be. So in order to know how you can grow, you must know the Lord and have His Power. I had been a born again Christian since the age of seventeen. I accepted the Lord in my life and was glad about it. I felt at this point everything was going to be perfect, not more problems and disappointments. Little did I know that this was when it all got started.

After college, I had no real chance to explore life or travel or be on my own. But little did I know, my biggest battle would come from not really seeking God. Something happened and I didn't realize what had taken place. Many things were revealed to me in the spirit realm that allowed my life to change forever.

For several years I took the blame for every problem that took place in my life. The enemy would send spirits to speak negative things to my mind that cut right to the bone. It was not until God gave me the strength to deal with the situation that I was able to go through and handle it. The more God elevates you to higher levels the more things won't hurt you as much. Through the Spirit, God allows things to happen to make you stronger.

At first I said "God, please don't let me go through this, anything but this." The Lord said no and that I could make it. No matter what, He had everything under control.

After coming into the realization, I knew that I had to take the enemy by force. I finally had to take action. God allowed me to journey to my family's home and never to return again.

It is often said, "To stay in the marriage No matter what . . ." and you believe every word of it; until your life is on the line. The enemy had plotted to mess up my mind.

God protected me at every angle (No weapon formed against me prospered) God didn't allow anything to harm me. I was 31 years old and ready to start my life over. With the help of the Word everyday I am asking for His guidance in what direction I need to go. God allowed me to flee the city where I could think and map my life out. I asked my Lord to, "Order my steps in Your Word."

In all of this I knew that God was a part of my life. God will always make a way of escape for His people.

I am a child of the King. God is making me, and God truly has My Back!

CHAPTER 6

The End of the Chapter/ The Beginning of a New

---

*I*t was a Friday after work, around four o'clock and I was on my way to the attorney office. This was the third visit to his office. All the way to the office my mind went all the way to my wedding day, how special it was. I could not believe that this was happening to me. At first, all I thought about was what the saints will think about me getting a divorce. How would they react to finding out that things could look so perfect on the outside, yet imperfect on the inside.

Before getting on the elevator, I prayed for God to give me the strength. I felt if God didn't strengthen me during this process, I would faint in the lawyer's office. As I got to the office, *Isaiah 14:10* came to mind.

*Behold, the Lord God will come with strong hand,
and his arm shall rule for him: behold, his reward
is with him, and his work before him.*

I felt the power of God, saying—"You can make
it." There is a time and season for everything. I
was there that day to start the divorce process. But
in my mind I knew that if there was any way possible, I would stay in the marriage. But God said
no! I asked God to release me from this situation,
from the battle that was against me. The Lord desires for His people to be free. I was never free spiritually or emotionally.

The enemy manifested and spoke to me stating
that before everything for me was over, the enemy
would have to be destroyed.

By not waiting on God for an answer, I had suffered more than I thought I could handle. However,
because I prayed to God for strength, He has blessed
and freed me from the battle that was against me.

During a Women's Conference, I spoke to a
group of women to tell them that there is going to
be a time when a trial comes, and only God can get
you through it. The enemy had a plan set up for me
in advance. The scripture says, "As a roaring lion,

he walks about seeking whom he may devour." If you are not careful Satan will step in and control your marriage, family and your life.

In my situation, the enemy used powers that the natural eye couldn't see. Unnatural use of the occult and the use of witchcraft can be used to harm your life. The enemy can use certain curses, which involved burying personal objects to insure harm to your life. God allowed me to identify whom the enemy was and what the enemy was trying to do to my life.

CHAPTER 7

Devil, I Identified You!

In your wildest dreams, you would not have believed what has happened to me. It was like opening a can of worms, to a snake but worse. Realizing the enemy was out seeking whom he may devour. My main intellect was to stay focused on God. I knew that I had to fight even more. Do you know what it is to have identified, someone working with the devil? I asked the Lord to show me my enemies. Why did I ask that question? God spoke and said—"there are many who will not be with you, and there are few who are with you. However, in the midst of identifying them, hold on, for I am only strengthening you for a purpose." You see, I didn't know why this was a pressure on my life. It was an episode. Everyday there were new episodes added onto my life. God is yet so awesome; He still kept me in the midst. The enemy will try to kill you softly. But it won't work. When reading this chapter, you might feel a little dampened on how the enemy works. You might feel angry; however keep an open mind so that you can allow yourself to get a good understanding.

During my life the enemy has tried to turn me away from God. I have experienced several traumatic events. Throughout the coarse of being single, experiencing a marriage, then a divorce, it has afforded me the opportunity to really know who God really is in my life. You can't always blame someone for your trials that you go through; given that God has allowed them to happen.

To women and men, have you ever wondered if you were married to the right soul mate and if God sent that person to you? At least I did! I thought I had everything made. I felt as though my life was complete. However, any marriage without God's approval and guidance will not last. In the duration of a marriage, many things can start to unfold. This will later lead to the destruction of your family. If you can blame anyone, I would blame the spirit of the devil, which manifests in people lives. Every woman wants their soul mate to be a lover and a friend. Believing that if this happen, this would be the end of the story. On the other hand, this is not the case. "My God from Zion, how are we deceived"! Your life can go from a dream to a nightmare. Many times you feel like an actress in a horror movie. Nevertheless, you're to never give up. God allowed me to stick it out until the very end.

Many times our greatest struggles start in the church. This situation provides an outline to whom you should marry and when to do it. I based my Christian walk on others, what they said was right, and not really acknowledging God's word for guidance. Women and men of God let us be wise and prudent in selecting our mate. Most importantly, let us study the Bible on marriage. So often we have overlooked what we've been taught outside of the word, we fail to notice that spirits or the spirit of Jezebel and Ahab are right in the church. These spirits rests in the church waiting and ready to destroy families. Repeatedly we are blind to what the devil is doing in the church.

Frequently we find ourselves missing the whole picture. Because a mask blinds us, things can happen right under our noses; and before we will acknowledge it we simply turn away. As Christians, we need to call, "a snake, a snake" and not be afraid to stand up for what is right. The devil will use people to get his job done. It does not matter what type of title you hold, you can be used by the devil. Whether you believe it or not, the devils ultimate goal is to use those that are closest to you. This will not only hurt you, but it will also destroy you without the God's protection.

You see we don't know whom the enemy has in place or his plans for attack. We never know how long the devil has plotted a plan upon your life. Nevertheless, we do know when God finally says, "Enough is enough, loose the coverings off your eyes." Traveling across the country, I have seen how the devil stepped in and destroyed a marriage, due to fleshly needs and wants. As a result, what looks good isn't always good for you. If you find yourself in a situation and you know your spouse is cheating or tipping in the tulips. Stand still, because God is still able to keep you. Always try to keep someone close to you, given that when you can't see, they can be eyes for you.

We find the spirit of Jezebel in the church walking around seeking whom it can devour. This spirit is bold and out spoken and refuses to be corrected in anyway. This type of spirit wants to control and destroy homes. This spirit will also, walk in the church and knock a preacher down to his knees.

God's people, please beware that this spirit is in the church. You must be required to always pray and fast. This will then allow you to identify the devil. Facing this spirit head on, I realize that without God, I couldn't defeat this enemy alone. Knowing that God has our back, the enemy has no means of having its way in our lives.

To the readers out there, it took all I could to write this chapter due to the pain and disappointments my life experienced. This is where I felt my life would end. But God said, "no," God had an investment in me, and I am to invest the purification, and sanctification of my soul. You have to be sold out for Jesus. Even though, these spirits operate in the church, they are able to use deception and become very trickery. Moreover, God always makes away of escape for his people.

In many ways the enemies know that their days are numbered. Yet, during the course of time, the enemy will use any human house that's not covered under the blood. In the church the spirit of Jezebel and Ahab's function is to play many games on God's people. The devil knows how to pick them. Yet, people say, "I am saved," but how is this so? My God, my God, you got to have our back! The spirit of Jezebel creeps into the church and seeks for its next victim. The desire of this spirit is to use demonic forces to attack God's people and take down anyone in its way. This spirit has skills that will kill everything that stands in his/her way.

Whether you realize it or not, the enemy has strategically mapped out what is intended for your life. The humor about the situation is that, he didn't understand that God had assigned angels to protect you. When men or women of God have fallen in the trap of the enemy, they fail to realize that they are not only hurting themselves, but those that are closest to them. During this process, the matters of life can be very painful. It goes from bad to worse. *Do you know what its like to have identified your enemy?* No matter how holy you say that you are, this trial is a difficult one. It feels like a deep wound that won't heal and a road of darkness with no light. I had no feelings and scales, which hindered me from seeing the destruction of my life; which blinded my eyes.

Accordingly, as true soldiers of God, keep focused and be aware of your surroundings in the church and in the home. In the home, be careful when lies are being told, the late nights out, never attending work and being spoken to in an aggressive manner. These are signs of the Jezebel spirit. Be very watchful in the actions of your love. Do not become shocked when you are told the truth. You might feel heartened to know that your relationship was based on lies. Continue your duties as a wife, husband or friend. Although it hurts, stand still and watch God make you strong.

Persistently in a relationship, we are deceived by our feelings. People set up plots against you. They also want to control and manipulate your life. Remember, in the home your life seems to be a horror movie and outside of the home it is a fantasy. This is where the frowns turn to smiles, the family portraits and the hugs and kisses. The devil likes to put on a show, so that it will lead the people to believe that life is sweet and that everything is okay.

On the other hand, your life is being played back and forth with a skillful spirit of the devil. The devil works with groups of people. He sets up holes for you to fall in. However, be sure to know that the same hole that you dig for me could be the hole for us. If you did one, you better did two!

Through all of the turmoil of life we must be able to stand on God's Word. Every time, I would minister the Word to God's people—somehow mess would break out. The devil does not like to be defeated. Many times during life trials, we must find ourselves getting away to spend time with God. I find my place of restoration in Georgia. Georgia is my hometown and is also my place of peace. There I am able to find my inner self and allow God to speak words of wisdom to my heart, mind and soul. At that time I knew that I had to get myself together.

CHAPTER 8

Church Affairs

This is the hardest chapter for me. Church was the very next place where the enemy made a bigger mess of things. The church is an institution that should provide peace and safety to a believer. We learn to trust the leadership and the members; however, when all our trust is placed in man we find ourselves idolizing leadership. With this, we are deceived and our thoughts are to make people into better gods that we worship. The church is the foundation of our Christian walk. The church is where we come to worship and fellowship. In addition, the church can even be a place that the enemy can enter and make a big mess, if allowed. You see, at the church we look at people as "Christian Folks" and believe that everything is "hunky-dory." When this happen we wear the masks of, "I have a happy family and everything is going well."

However, in the home some of us are faced to live with a person, who is controlled by a demonic force or spirit. Many times men and women play roles of being married, yet their desire is to be single. We then will start pretending to be something or someone that we are not. In doing so, strong leaders in the church are tricked by the enemy's plans. I recall learning a story of how a power preacher, who was taken down by the Jezebel spirit. This Jezebel spirit slithered into the church, like a snake. Without a strong prayer life, this spirit can with no trouble destroy a congregation into small pieces. This spirit has a purpose to come and rattle the "saints" and "aints" of God. We shouldn't be afraid, but be assured that God still and will always have our back. At the time, we don't always see the spirit for what it is worth. Many times, jealousy can be as cruel as the grave. However, as Christians, jealousy should not be named among us. Henceforth, we need to know that these spirits lurk around the vicinity of where you worship. Placing a spirit of fear in your heart, will give you a scary feeling that seems to overshadow you.

I realized that I could not let the enemy stop me from worshipping or going to church. I knew that I had to pray much harder. However, every function that happen at church, there was the enemy. When this occurred, I wanted to give up! I remember experiencing this feeling in the church, not sure what to do and I couldn't understand why? Through all of this, God was yet covering my back. With all understanding, I knew that the enemy operates through this spirit, which deals heavily in demonic forces. This trail in the church leads me to believe that even when there is an assignment to destroy your life, God steps in again to cover your pathway. The assignments went from doing rituals to placing objects in the ground. This is what you can call, an assassination in place to take your life.

Do you understand what I am trying to say? It is the enemy's ultimate goal to kill you. The enemy will also try to kill the saints in the church. Through all of this, we must continue to preach the gospel. You see, in the church the enemy never wants to see you prosper; they only want the "spotlight to shine on them." In doing so, the focused is removed from God and placed on man. In the church we find witches and warlocks operating in full numbers. This is what dealing in witchcraft will do. As Christians we must also be aware of how so called Christians start wearing satanic jewelry. The items include jewelry such as, chain bracelets, rings, and necklaces. When wearing such items, beware of demonic forces.

I recall being forced with really understanding what these items meant. These forces can be found in the church. You see, many can fool the people, but you can't fool God. When plans and plots are set up in large groups; keep your spiritual eyes open. I remember experiencing the voice of God directing me not to eat or drink during a gathering. He stated to me that this could and may be harmful to me. At that time, I knew God had my back. He will provide protection for His own. Believe it or not, this all took place after being asked to preach during a service. I did not know I had to speak until I was asked.

However, I did preach and God moved abundantly, and has to this day. The message was, "Killing It At the Root." I believe that if it had not been for the anointing, God would not have opened my eyes to the dangers that entailed me. How could demons work through the lives of Christians and how could we be so naïve of a Jezebel spirit. Believe it or not, Witchcraft is so powerful, but not powerful enough to overtake God.

Looking how the church is set up the enemy can influence or tap into the leaders. This happens through witchcraft or an occult. This will place you in the mouth of demons. You must stand and say, "Lord, here I am I present myself to you." No matter what, God always has your back. Therefore, no matter what plan or plot, God will step in on time.

> *But thanks be to God, which giveth us the victory through our Lord Jesus Christ.* (1 Corinthians 15:57)

This lets you know that God will always give you the victory. The Lord ordains peace to his people. After this experience I knew that demons work through the lives of people. You know what is possible and what can happen. Witchcraft is powerful, but God's power is totally in control. The Lord always wins His battles.

CHAPTER 9

Where Do I Go from Here?

In the midst of this situation I lost so very much. I lost my church, my home and my family due to what was brought against me. But even through each situation God manifested Himself. The first Sunday that I didn't go to church, I searched the city trying to find a place to worship. The Lord allowed me to come into contact with different leaders to stand in the gap for me. The Lord always has somebody ready to stand with you when you're in His Will.

> *I will hear what God the Lord will speak: for he will speak peace unto his people, and to his saints: but let them not turn again to folly.* (Psalm 85:8)

The Lord will give peace unto his people. If it were not for the peace of God, I would not have survived such a devastating experience. During the waiting period, the Lord allowed me to strengthen my spirit. This took place through prayer and studying His Word. Each day I felt myself growing more and more. I became stronger in God.

CHAPTER 10

Peace That Passeth All Understanding

───── ❧ ─────

*I*know when you reach this place in reading this book, perhaps in your mind you're thinking: how can she have survived? Where did she find peace? To begin with, let's define peace. . . . In Webster's Dictionary, peace is defined as: 1. Freedom from war, fighting 2. Law and order 3. Calm or quiet. This is what man's meaning of peace is, however, the Bible says in *Philippians 4:7*:

> *And the peace of God, which passeth all under standing, shall keep your hearts and minds through Christ Jesus.*

In understanding this particular scripture we must understand that through every trial in our lives, it is clear that if we depend on God, He will give peace not like the world, but peace that passeth all understanding. This means that the Lord is there, even though I am going through a hard trial, I can still lift up the Lord. Blessing His name at all times. But the most important key is that I don't even understand myself, while shouting to the Glory of God. Tears are falling, my heart is broken, and the pain seems unbearable, but I am still going to PRAISE GOD. When we reach this level on this journey, we begin to realize that Spiritual growth is taking place, and the peace of God is ruling your heart.

God deals with us through faith and complete trust in Him. As people of God, He wants us to rely on Him and the Word.

Peace I leave with you, my peace I give unto you: not as the world giveth, give I unto you. Let not your heart be troubled, neither let it be afraid. (John 14:27)

God wants us not to worry about anything, no matter how it looks. Notice what the Bible says in *Philippians 4:6–7:*

Be careful for nothing; but in every thing by prayer and supplication with thanksgiving let your requests be made known unto God. And the peace of

*God, which passeth all understanding, shall keep
your hearts and minds through Christ Jesus.*

This is the believer's assurance that even though
it looks like I am losing the battle, I have "perfect
peace" in the Word of God. No matter what you
may go through, God wants you to know that we
have confidence in Him and His Power. Are you willing to trust Me and seek My peace? Are you willing
to leave all to keep Me? These are questions God is
asking you right now.

Based on these questions you can declare to yourself, I will have peace. We must tell ourselves this
daily and you will have the peace of God. I found
myself listening to a tape my sister purchased for
me "The Morning Glory" by Prophetess Bynum. In
all honesty I listen to this tape every morning. The
songs were so powerful; it ministered to the depth
of my spirit. The Lord will deliver you from every
battle that is against you when you give every thing
over to Him.

Sometime we might say, Lord, but it hurts and I
can't find any peace in this battle. The apostle Paul
told Timothy that God had a purpose in all the heart-
aches and sufferings. It doesn't always stop when
we want it to be over and I know it doesn't feel good,

but God, there has to be a reason for this battle that I am faced with in my life.

> *For the which cause I also suffer these things: nevertheless I am not ashamed: for I know whom I have believed, and am persuaded that he is able to keep that which I have committed unto him against that day.* (2 Timothy 1:12)

What am I saying? Many times, to develop "perfect peace," God allows us to go through some things so that we can recognize that we need Him, and that without Him we would fail. If you never have trials or problems, you never need a problem solver. The more you need Him, the more you have to call Him. The best part in all of this is the more you call on Him, the more God shows up. He steps in on your behalf and makes that problem get right. The more He steps in the better you trust and know Him. That's the ultimate goal: "We must know Him in order to find peace." At this time in my life, I have found Jesus Christ as a Provider. I know Him as a Protector. I know Him as a Keeper. I know Him as a Healer. I know Him as a Mind Regulator. He kept me. He gave me peace. The Lord watched out for me even when I thought I could do it myself. The peace that I have gotten in my heart did not come from the world. God knows how much you can bear, and He knows how much you can handle.

In your continuous strive to see God when this life is over, God removes obstacles out of your life that hinder you from having perfect peace when you trust Him. One thing we can count on about God is that He will not leave you in limbo without giving you purpose. This depends on if we continue to keep His peace.

CHAPTER 11

Waiting on Him

*M*any times we are in battles because it is the wrong time and the wrong place where we find ourselves. So often we react out of God's Will because we want to know when God will move. Most of the time we don't have enough patience to wait on God.

God wants me to tell you to wait on Him until your change comes. If you don't wait, the enemy will stab you in your back. You can't see behind your back, therefore we need God.

Don't let the enemy trick you into thinking that you "got it going on." Just when you think you are safe, he steps into view. The Lord says in *Revelation 2:2–5*:

I know thy works, and thy labour, and thy patience, and how thou canst not bear them which are evil: and thou hast tried them which say they are apostles, and are not, and hast found them liars:

And hast borne, and hast patience, and for my name's sake hast laboured, and hast not fainted.

Nevertheless I have somewhat against thee, because thou hast left thy first love.

Remember therefore from whence thou art fallen, and repent, and do the first works; or else I will come unto thee quickly, and will remove thy candlestick out of his place, except thou repent.

You started off just fine. You did what you were asked to do in the church. You fasted and prayed. But for some reason the enemy was able to offer you something to let you out of the Will of God. God lets us know, "I told you I would bless and care for you," but something got your attention. When your attention is divided and you can't stay focused on God because your mind is somewhere else, this tells you that "you have left your first love."

If the enemy can get you to stop looking to God, he can change your heart. If contingent on the orientation of your heart, this will determine if God will give you the desires of your heart. God doesn't get alarmed when something gets out of control, because He is all knowing. He knows the end from the beginning. God allows things to mess up in our lives so we can see where we are in Him.

> *And I appoint unto you a kingdom, as my Father hath appointed unto me;*
>
> *That ye may eat and drink at my table in my kingdom, and sit on thrones judging the twelve tribes of Israel.*
>
> *And the Lord said, Simon, Simon, behold, Satan hath desired to have you, that he may sift you as wheat:*
>
> *But I have prayed for thee, that thy faith fail not: and when thou art converted, strengthen thy brethren.* (Luke 22:29–32)

It is clear the enemy hates you, and he never takes a break always on the job. Jesus told Simon "Satan hath desired to have you, but I prayed for you." This is the message I want to stress to the body of Christ, the devil wants to get intimate with you so he can take advantage of your life. Your enemy is cunning and wants you to comprise your position in God. He watches and waits for the right time to attack. The first time you drop your guard, get ready, he is going to manipulate your every move. Many times we underestimate the enemy. Just because you win a battle that does not mean that the devil is through. If we are not sure about something, he makes it a hindrance. Satan desires to sift you. He does not act at one time, the enemy does it slowly. You don't really notice it until a significant amount of your life is taken. What do you mean? You are still preaching, singing and dancing, but your anointing is running out. As Christians, we must wait on the anointing of God because that is what breaks every yoke. Remember David was anointed to be king over Israel, but he was not ready to reign yet. In order to have power you must wait on God.

David was anointed as a youth, but that wasn't his time to be king. My connection with David is that even though God was in my life at an early age, just like David, my season had not arrived. We must keep working until our time comes.

God allows tests to come in our life to prepare us for the giant. David proved that he could battle. He fought a lion and a bear before he confronted Goliath. Are you willing to prepare for your final test? If you wait on God, like David, the Lord will make sure you are ready.

And David said unto Saul, Thy servant kept his father's sheep, and there came a lion, and a bear, and took a lamb out of the flock:

And I went out after him, and smote him, and de-livered it out of his mouth: and when he arose against me, I caught him by his beard, and smote him, and slew him. Thy servant slew both the lion and the bear: and this uncircumcised Philistine shall be as one of them, seeing he hath defied the armies of the living God. David said moreover, The Lord that delivered me out of the paw of the lion, and out of the paw of the bear, he will de-liver me out of the hand of this Philistine. And Saul said unto David, Go, and the Lord be with thee. (1 Samuel 17:34–37)

CHAPTER 12

Paying a High Price

$\mathcal{I}$ realize today there's a price for any position in God. Many times I cried, "Where are you God?" What happened to all the kind words? The prophecies? The time of transformation is difficult and it hurts . . . but one day the hurt changed into a level of God I could not believe. This level went beyond flesh.

In my transformation, I had to "tarry" the old time away. This is when you don't care how you look. Your voice is gone and your knees are hurting because you are praying all the time. When your level is reached, the Spirit will validate you, and not the person.

A revelation given to me was, who you are in God will always contradict who men say that you are. That's why the Bible says "Woe unto you when all men shall speak well of you" (Luke 6:26). When you find that you are pleasing men, there must be something about you that's not pleasing God.

That's why I have suffered humiliation; people I thought I really knew began to question my devotion to God. I had to hear "She'll never be anything. She's not thinking spiritual." I had once had popularity in my church, which felt good, however this was not the most important thing I needed to have in my life. It had gotten to the point that people I believe and trusted in turned their backs on me. The Lord showed me the ones I thought were with me, were also against me.

In all of this I prayed to God to give me a true ministry. One, which would be a burden to the people, just like, Ezekiel had talked about. In doing this, my heart was able to forgive my enemy because where God's heart goes, my heart went, also. I started to care for the soul and not only the flesh.

The Lord gave me a hurting of the flesh letting me know that we need to have the love of God in us. I found myself with an agenda but a strong will to please God. God has a will and a way that will be done in our lives.

> *To every thing there is a season, and a time to every purpose under the heaven:*
>
> *A time to be born and a time to die; a time to plant, and a time to pluck up that which is planted;* (Ecclesiastes 3:1–2)

Solomon, the wisest man who ever lived, encouraged us to respect the seasons of our lives. When God say, "Go," you have to move. We must believe that the safest place in the world is in the Will of God.

I have found out that going this way, everyone is not meant to like you. You will not be the apple of everyone's eyes. People will not always understand you. So stop trying to please them. Many times, people that you have in your circle are not a part of the purpose that God has for your life. When you find that something is not a part of your purpose, cut it loose. Notice the story of Gideon; he fulfilled his call to deliver Israel from the Midianites. God cut the men to only the amount he needed to defeat the enemy.

*And the Lord said unto Gideon, The people that
are with thee are too many for me to give the
Midianites into their hands, lest Israel vaunt themselves against me, saying, Mine own hand hath
saved me.*

*Now therefore go to, proclaim in the ears of the
people, saying, Whosoever is fearful and afraid,
let him return and depart early from Mount Gilead.
And there returned of the people twenty and two
thousand; and there remained ten thousand.*
(Judges 7:2–3)

Each time the Lord said to Gideon, "You have
too many people in your entourage to fulfill my purpose, then cut out the crowd around you." If you
have friends that are not a part of God's purpose
during your season, they have to go out of your life.
Many times so-called friends don't have your best
interest at heart. They serve no purpose but to use
you for their needs, that is not a friend. God will
allow a peaceful parting, if you take heed to the
warning. Gideon gave the men a reason to leave and
said that it would be all right if they did so.

Those who left at that time served the purpose
in Gideon's life. Don't feel that everybody will hurt
too much when you leave. Get ready to bid them a
fond farewell and go on with your life in God.

This was very difficult to grasp, you mean people I had known for thirteen or fourteen years? The Lord said, "Yes." Their purpose in your life is done.

CHAPTER 13

If God Says "Go"

So stop and think. Many times God tells us to cut certain people, leave jobs, and get out of certain relationships, but we fail to obey Him. This can be easy to do while God is giving you time. God knows how to make it easy for you. If you wait, it could get harder. Look at what happened to Gideon.

And the Lord said unto Gideon, The people are yet too many; bring them down unto the water, and I will try them for thee there: and it shall be, that of whom I say unto thee, This shall go with thee, the same shall go with thee; and of whomsoever I say unto thee, This shall not go with thee, the same shall not go. (Judges 7:4)

You need people who can put something into your spiritual life. The Lord will put people in your life that will administer help to you during your seasons. This is sure because He has put me in the place with so many wonderful and knowledgeable people of God that aided me in my battle. If I had remained in the same place, I would not have been prepared.

You have to consider that these people that you are cutting out of your life are not a part of God's divine Will, they were destroying what God had for me. Many times we don't need friends. Yes I said "friends." You need to have a covenant relationship with the people in your life.

Greater love hath no man than this, that a many lay down his life for his friends. (John 15:13)

My reason for saying this is that a covenant relationship with a friend means that our relationship is stronger than death. I am going to be there through the good times and bad times. When Jesus stated true friends are willing to give themselves up for you, that's a covenant. When I began to look at my friends, I found that even though it looked as though I had so many, in reality, I had a few. The few are the kind of people I needed in my life.

I the Lord have called thee in righteousness, and will hold thine hand, and will keep thee, and give thee for a covenant of the people, for a light of the Gentiles. (Isaiah 42:6)

Then God sends a person, they will be with you through the storms in your life. This person is commissioned by God to assist you. I remember telling my sister to leave now because the battle I was in was going to be rough. I began to focus on not having time for people who God had not sent into my life. I thought about questions that would help me stay in check with people that entered my life:

- Did God send you my way?

- Are you in my life to help me reach my goals?

But the bottom line is to reach my goal. God continued to protect me in finding my friends.

CHAPTER 14

The Word Brought Me through

The most important weapon we have is the Word from the Lord. I totally depend on the Word of the Lord, because if it's in the Word, I can find a hiding place. Many times I ran to this one and that one, but when it came down to it, all I needed was the Word.

> Neither have I gone back from the commandment of his lips; I have esteemed the words of his mouth more than my necessary food. (Job 23:12)

The word of God is the breath of life, and without it we would die. I found myself eating the word for lunch, snack, and for dinner. I made it a part of my every day life. I had my Bible everywhere. At work, at home, in the bathroom, anywhere possible, I had the Word of God.

Your success in God depends on your life in the
Word. You must stay in the Word, which would allow God to protect you at all times. God just won't
keep, without some effort and dedication on your
part. Jesus taught us the relationship between the
Word and truth.

> *Then said Jesus to those Jews, which believed, on
> him, if ye continue in my word, then are ye my
> disciples indeed;*
>
> *And ye shall know the truth, and the truth shall
> make you free.* (John 8:31,32)

If you continue in the Word, you will be His
disciples and know how to stay free. When I found
myself going to church, knowing that I was going
to get something spiritually, the Word came alive.
Because when you have the Word, you want to be
tossed about with every wind of doctrine. When you
know the Word of God, and something comes up
that's not like Him, you can dismiss this trick and
not fall prey to the enemy.

> *Though the Lord be high, yet hath he respect unto
> the lowly: but the proud he knoweth afar off.*
>
> *Though I walk in the midst of trouble, thou wilt
> revive me: thou shalt stretch forth thine hand*

against the wrath of mine enemies, and thy right hand shall save me.

The Lord will perfect that which concerneth me: Thy mercy, O Lord, endureth forever:

Forsake not the works of thine own hands. (Psalms 136:6–8)

Even though I am in trouble, I know that your words say you will stand up against my enemy. My mind goes back to a six o'clock prayer meeting, when Missionary Wright began to quote the Word of God. After that night, because the Word was so powerful, I could hear the words she quoted in my ear and the Word of God cut right through to the bone. It reached down to my inner man and took root. The Word of God is Powerful.

CHAPTER 15

Conclusion: Know Your Choice

All I ever wanted was to be real for God. The Apostle Paul says in 1 Timothy 4:14–15:

> *Neglect not the gift that is in thee, which was given thee by prophecy, with the laying on of the hands of the presbytery.*

> *Meditate upon these things; give thyself wholly to them, that thy profiting may appear to all.*

When a prophecy is told to you, god will confirm it through His Word. A true prophet of God brings to your life a word from God that can change your experience. If it is of God, He will give you some signs. Paul's prophecy would profit many. That meant that people will be edified through your work

95

in God. God uses whom He wants to use, whenever He wants to use them. I strongly believe that God chose me in my mother's womb. The Bible states in *Matthew 20:16*:

> *So the last shall be first, and the first last: for many are called, but few chosen.*

This is what Jesus Himself said, that many people have a call on their life, but only a few will complete what God has called them to do. When I entered the realm of the Chosen, the Lord had put me at a level in Him to produce and help bring souls to Christ.

One Sunday while setting in church, a minister who didn't know me, said the Spirit told him to call me out to sing a solo. I began to sing the song "I Won't Complain" and the Lord poured out a blessing in the church. Unknowingly, a young woman who was sitting in the church, had kidney failure. Two weeks later, I received a letter from her stating how the song gave her strength to go on. In this the Lord let me know that even though my trials seem to be taking over, His Spirit was in me. I had to put self out of the way to be a blessing to someone else.

*Then the word of the Lord came unto me, saying,
Before I formed thee in the belly I knew thee; and
before thou camest forth out of the womb I sanctified thee, and I ordained thee a prophet unto the
nations.* (Jeremiah 1:4–5)

The point is clear. The Lord said to Jeremiah that
not only did He know him, but also He knew him
before he was born. This meant He set him apart, or
chose him. The Lord ordains and approves His chosen vessels. When you are chosen, God puts your
life into motion and He's in complete control. This
was true for me because I never received a license
to preach, it just happened. Man did not give me
approval, it came from God.

*Ye have not chosen me, but I have chosen you, and
ordained you, that ye should go and bring forth
fruit, and that your fruit should remain: that what-
soever ye shall ask of the Father in my name, he
may give it to you.* (John 15:16)

However, Bishop Harvey D. Bryan, Sr., *Prelate of
Western Florida Jurisdiction*, licensed me as an ordained Evangelist in the Church of God In Christ.
When I committed my life over to God, I was on
God's agenda. I had to disregard everything that was
familiar to me. The church, my job and my family
in order for God to use me. You devote yourself to

God whole-heartedly and engulf yourself in His Word until you get answers from Him. The outcome is knowing the perfect Will of God for your life. In your preparation, beware of assigned demons that will come to hinder you. The come to take every-thing out of your Spirit that God has placed there. In order to defeat this enemy, you must continue to kill the flesh. The enemy feeds on the flesh, don't let your ego stand in the way, "Starve the flesh and feed the Spirit."

In being chosen by God, I had to realize what was His Will in my life. The road seemed so dark, but yet He became my light. At this stage of my life, I am willing to endure anything to keep God as my protector. He has healed my broken heart, loosed my spirit, gave me my mind back, and gave me His power. In doing these things for me, I am a better person inside and outside.

When you wait on the Lord, be of good cour-age, He will direct your path. You pay a price for being chosen by God, but in the end it's all worth it. In the midst of everything, I often relied on verse *Psalm 136:6–8:*

To him that stretched out the earth above the wa-ters: for his mercy endureth forever. To him that made

*great lights: for his mercy endureth forever: The sun
to rule by day: for his mercy endureth forever.*

He protected me from the battle that was
against me.

The Lord declared it was my time to come forth.
Doors and ways were going to open up for me if I
stayed in His Will. All I want to do is embrace the
blessings of God through His Word.

No matter what you are facing in your life, re-
member "God's Got Your Back," so hold on. Jesus
Christ is the best protector you can have. The Holy
Spirit can and will abide in you!

A Parting Word

After reading this book, I challenge you to believe in God for complete protection by His Spirit.
So remember no matter how bad a situation is going, just know "God's Got Your Back." God sees and
knows everything in your life before it happens.

God's Got Your Back!

Special Thanks

My Lord and Savior Jesus Christ

- Bishop Harvey D. Bryan, Sr. Western Florida Jurisdiction Prelate

- Missionary Almarie Bryan First Lady of Holy Redeemer COGIC

- The late Mother Alice Curry Greensboro, North Carolina

- Mrs. Brilela "Granny" Taylor Houston, Texas

- Sister in Christ, Sharon

- Holy Redeemer COGIC Family

Thanks Be to God for Having Your Spiritual Guidance in My Life

To order additional copies of

God's
GOT YOUR
Back

Have your credit card ready and call:
1-877-421-READ (7323)
or please visit our web site at

www.pleasantword.com
Also available at: www.amazon.com

CPSIA information can be obtained at www.ICGtesting.com
Printed in the USA
LVOW061855070212

267544LV00001B/172/A

A PRELIMINARY EXPLANATION:

Holy Thursday, Good Friday, the Holy Saturday Easter Vigil, and Easter Sunday are all one extended celebration of Easter called the "Easter Triduum" (three days from Thursday evening to Sunday evening). So we begin the Easter season with reflections on Holy Thursday, the beginning of the Easter celebration.

During the Easter Season we will draw from the Mass readings whatever casts light on our baptismal consecration as *prophets*. This is the season to open ourselves to the Holy Spirit and the promise of "power from on high" that comes with the "Gift of the Spirit." We will do this by putting a particular focus on the part of the Mass which corresponds most to this call and commitment to prophetic witness: the *Presentation of Gifts*.[1]

The *Presentation of Gifts* is an important, but under-appreciated moment in the Eucharistic Celebration. It should be a moment of intense re-affirmation of our baptismal commitment and of our conscious desire to participate fully and actively in the mission of the Church. In practice, however, it is often treated almost like a "time-out" in the action of the Mass while the ministers do some table-setting.

The instructions for celebrating Eucharist in the Roman rite direct that after the *Liturgy of the Word* an "acolyte [server] or other lay minister arranges the corporal, purificator, the chalice, the pall, and the missal upon the altar."[2] After this the bread and wine are brought to the altar, and the presiding priest *presents* them to the assembly and to God. The gifts will not be truly *offered* until, during the *Eucharistic Prayer* they, and we with them, are offered as the Body and Blood of Christ. What the *Presentation of Gifts* makes clear is that the bread and wine represent everyone present; that we will be present in the host that is offered at Mass, just as Baptism made us present in the body of Christ offered on the cross.

Before the presider presents the wine, he pours a little water into it from a "cruet." Afterwards he washes his hands to make them clean before touching the bread and wine he will be giving to people in Communion.

If all this is done by the presiding priest and altar servers alone at the altar, the congregation hardly seems to be involved. All the more so if a hymn is being sung while the presider presents the gifts to God, because in that case the presider says the accompanying prayers "inaudibly." If it is done right, however, two or more of the faithful will carry the gifts up from the back of the church, passing through the whole congregation, and put them in the hands of the presider, who will place them on the altar. The *Instruction* provides that the hymn can be terminated when the gifts reach the altar, in which case the prayers are said audibly so that the congregation can hear and enter into what they are expressing.

Properly done, the *Presentation of Gifts* is filled with meaning. It is the Catholic equivalent of a Baptist "altar call" when, after the preaching, the minister invites all those who want to "give themselves to Jesus" to come forward. This is a

1

public, adult expression of personal response to the Gospel and of commitment to serve as a follower of Jesus. Catholics are invited to reaffirm their Baptism in every Mass.

The gifts represent us. The *Instruction* says it is "most desirable" that there be the same number of hosts brought up as there are people present at Mass. And they should be brought up through the whole congregation. Thus every person present is able to "go forward" symbolically, represented by a host, to be placed on the altar.

The bread and wine are placed there to be transformed into the body and blood of Christ. We whom they represent have already been transformed into Christ's body by Baptism. But we put ourselves on the altar again with the bread and wine as a way of saying three things: first that we *want* to be the body of Christ. We reaffirm the Baptism that made us his body and commit to being so. Second, we put ourselves on the altar as a declaration we are putting ourselves personally into the Mass and into all the mystery it expresses. Third, we are putting ourselves on the altar to be *changed*—not into Christ's body and blood, since we already are that by Baptism—but asking the Father to "bring the image of your Son to perfection within us." This is a commitment to *continuing conversion.*[3]

Each one is called to enter personally and intensely into this moment of the Mass, using "affective prayer"—that is, just *desiring*: for example, *offering* oneself, fervently *willing* to be, to become, or to do what is consciously in one's heart. And at the end of the *Presentation of Gifts* the presider invites us to put our commitment into words. At the invitation, "Pray, brothers and sisters, that our sacrifice may be acceptable to God, the almighty Father," we come to our feet and respond.

"*May the Lord accept the sacrifice*"—the sacrifice we are all offering, but through "your hands." We offer it. We choose to. First, "*for the praise and glory of his name.*" That was our focus during the *Introductory Rites*. Second, "*for our good.*" This is the way we listened during the *Liturgy of the Word*—as *disciples*, determined to "get something out of it." And finally, "*for the good of all his Church.*" We are here, not just to receive, but to give. We dedicate ourselves to "building up the Church" as committed adults. We accept as our own the Church's *mission* to the world, according to our baptismal consecration as *prophets, priests,* and *stewards of his kingship.*[4]

If we enter into the Easter Season with a desire to open ourselves to the Spirit and give ourselves to the mission of Christ we will find help in these *Reflections*. They will show us how to let the Mass remind, teach, and encourage us to live lives of *prophetic witness.*

---

[1] *Luke* 24:48-49; *Acts* 1:8.
[2] See the *General Instruction on the Roman Missal* propagated by the National Conference of Catholic Bishops, 2002. See especially paragraphs 51, 73-76, 85, 139, 141-142.
[3] *Romans* 6:3. See Lenten Preface I.
[4] See *1Corinthians* 13:11; 4:12, 20, 26; *Ephesians* 4:11-16.

APRIL 21, 2011

Mass of the Lord's Supper

The *Responsorial* is: *"The cup of bless-ing that we bless, is it not a sharing in the blood of Christ?"* (*1Corinthians* 10:16). *Psalm* 116 elaborates on it.

The "Easter triduum" consists of three days that constitute one single celebra-tion. Any one of them without the oth-ers is incomplete.

The *Easter Vigil* celebrates the resur-rection of Jesus as the mystery that gives meaning to all human life and history. But without the celebration of Christ's sacrificial death on *Good Fri-day*, Easter would be unintelligible. And without the institution of the Eu-charist, celebrated on *Holy Thursday*, Christ's death and resurrection would be a thing of the past—reported, re-membered, and relied upon—but present only to God in the transcen-dent "Now" of eternity; not present to us in the time and place of the world we live in. Taken together, the three days reveal Christian life as an individ-ual and communal presence to and participation in the ongoing act of love by which the Father, Son, and Spirit re-deemed the world. The *Liturgy of the Word* is to help us understand this mystery. We listen to the readings as *disciples* eager to learn.

Exodus 12:1-14: "This month shall stand at the head of your calendar." Time counts, and we should count time, not just numerically by adding hours and days, but historically, seeing it as a series of events. The events are what give time meaning. By celebrat-ing events we absorb their meaning into our lives and pass that meaning on to others.

The readings that are part of the cele-bration do three things: they *tell the story* of the events, *remind* us to keep them in memory, and *explain* to us their meaning. Where the meaning is expressed in symbols, the readings tell us what those symbols say.

Reading God's word is always part of our celebration. It lets us understand what we celebrate. Celebration makes what is proclaimed or taught in the word real and active in our lives—es-pecially our communal lives. Liturgy unites light to life and us to one an-other in the "communion of the Holy Spirit."

1Corinthians 11:23-26 is an example: the words present the mystery "handed on" to us. But we *proclaim* it as a com-munity every time we "eat this bread and drink this cup."

In **John 13:1-15** Jesus teaches us how to participate in Mass. *"Do you realize what I have done?"* It is not enough to see and hear; we have to *think*, medi-tate, absorb the meaning of the words, gestures, and symbols. And keep doing it: "You may not realize now what I am doing, but later you will understand." Hearing should prompt personal re-flection and communal discussion.

And we have to *act* on what we hear: "As I have done, so you must do." Hear-ing should lead to *decisions*. Jesus is both "Teacher" and "Lord." His words are not just data; they are *directions*—to be acted on.

Initiative: Don't leave Mass without making a *decision* based on what you heard.

3

APRIL 22, 2011

The *Responsorial* (*Psalm* 31) expresses the choice our whole lives should lead to: *"Father, into your hands I commend my spirit."* The readings show us the faith, hope, and love we need to do it.

Both **Isaiah 52:13 to 53:12** and **Hebrews 4:14 to 5:9** are reflections on the **Passion Narrative, John 18:1 to 19:42**. *Isaiah* looks ahead to it; *Hebrews* looks back on it. Both are meditations.

Isaiah tells us Jesus' life had value "because he surrendered himself to death." The same is true of ours. By "dying" in Baptism to everything life on this earth offers and promises, we entered into Life. But we have to *live out* that death.

In this fourth and last "Song of the Servant," Isaiah says the life of Jesus and his followers is shocking. He says, "Who would believe...?" People will be "amazed," "startled," turned off. "There was in him no appearance that would attract us to him. He was spurned and avoided... We held him in no esteem." But read Isaiah's text and then *Psalm* 31. The way God used and rewarded Christ's life leads us to say, *"Father, into your hands I commend my spirit."*

Hebrews tells us why we no longer hold Jesus "in no esteem." He is our lifeline to God and beatitude, "Jacob's ladder," connecting heaven to earth.[1]

Hebrews invites us to reflect on what Jesus is as "priest." Jesus is the "connector." The bridge. He is not just a third-party mediator or intercessor, standing alongside us and the Father. Through Jesus we are *connected* to the Father. He mediates God's life to us by bringing us into God and God into us. He intercedes for us from within our hearts. He doesn't just pray for us, he prays *as* us, and we pray as him. Through our identification with him by Baptism we are "priests in the Priest."[2]

Even psychologically, we can "connect" with Jesus because he is not "unable to sympathize with our weakness." He was "tempted in every way that we are." The bottom of the ladder is stuck in our earth. We can get our feet on it.

On earth, when Jesus was "in the flesh, he offered prayers and supplications with loud cries and tears"—just like us. And he "learned obedience from what he suffered." But now that he is "made perfect," he has become "the source of eternal salvation for all who obey him."

The top of the ladder is in heaven. Jesus is "a great high priest who has passed through the heavens, Jesus the Son of God." Jesus connects us to God.

Obedience is the key. Jesus was "made perfect" in obedience to the Father. We are made perfect by obeying the Father "through him, with him, and in him," in surrendered union with Jesus as members of his body responsive to our Head. In life and in death we say as he says in us: *"Father, into your hands I commend my spirit."*[3]

Now read the **Passion Narrative**.

[1] See *Genesis* 28:10-22 and *John* 1:45-51.
[2] See *John* 14:9-20; 16:23-28.
[3] See *Ephesians* 5:21-30; *Philippians* 3:7-21; *Colossians* 1:11-24; 2:6 to 3:4.

Initiative: Spend your life saying, *"Father, into your hands I commend my spirit."*

APRIL 23, 2011

The liturgy teaches us to meditate on the word of God by giving us examples of meditation. One of the most all-inclusive meditations on the mystery and gift of the death and resurrection of Jesus is the *Exsultet* or "Easter Proclamation."

First the presiding priest lights the Easter candle from the new fire that was kindled in darkness at the doors of the church as a symbol of the new light Jesus brought into the world. He prays in the name of all: "May the light of Christ, rising in glory, dispel the darkness of our hearts and minds." The victory of Christ is a victory of Truth over error. His light is the "light of life."

God's word is a light to "walk in." We reflect on God's word as *disciples* to find in it a "way of life." This Light is indistinguishable from the Life of Christ, and it is only "in Christ" as sharers in his divine life by grace, that we can see and understand: "For with you is the fountain of life; in your light we see light."[1]

The priest or deacon processes through the church, carrying the Easter candle. Three times he stops, lifts the candle high, and sings, *"Christ our Light!"* The people respond, *"Thanks be to God!"* This is a proclamation of faith and commitment that affirms our *identity* as Christians. We are the people who have chosen the light of Christ to be our light rather than the darkness of human culture. We recognize his teaching as a gift. We are grateful for it.

The "gift of the Holy Spirit" we associate with Baptism is *Understanding*. The "fruit of the Spirit" is *Joy*. This is the Light that is Life.[2]

EASTER JOY

The first theme of the *Exsultet* is "Rejoice!"

Rejoice, heavenly powers! Sing, choirs of angels! Exult, all creation around God's throne. Jesus Christ, our King, is risen. Rejoice O earth… glory fills you…

Because Christ "has risen… has conquered… darkness vanishes forever."

Rejoice O Mother Church! Exult in glory…. Let this place resound with joy.

If we cannot resonate with that, we have not heard the Good News. We need to immerse ourselves in discipleship, absorbing the message of the Gospel.

The *Exsultet* now summarizes what the Good News is. It concentrates our attention on the five basic mysteries, promises, and commitments of Baptism.

A NEW IDENTITY

Christians everywhere, washed clean of sin and freed from all defilement, are restored to grace….

This is the mystery that includes all others: our *transformation* from slaves of sin into free children of the Father through the *new identity* that is ours. By incorporation into his body on the cross, dying and rising in him, we have "become Christ."

Christ has ransomed us with his blood and paid the price of Adam's sin…

A price, not of punishment due, but of ransom from servitude to "the world, the flesh, and the devil." Because "Christ, the true Lamb is slain," we died in him, our sins were annihilated, and we rose as his body, a "new creation," blessed with the very "holiness of God."[3]

5

ENLIGHTENMENT

This is the night when the pillar of fire destroyed the darkness of sin.

The mystery of this transformation is that we are now the "light of the world." We enjoy the *enlightenment* promised to those who commit themselves as *disciples*, students of the word of God.

> If you continue in my word, you are truly my disciples; and you will know the truth, and the truth will make you free."[4]

POWER IN THE SPIRIT

Freedom has a purpose. The delivered have a destiny.

> *You freed the people of Israel from their slavery and led them dry-shod through the sea.*

The Red Sea was a symbol and preview of Baptism. By passing through its waters the Chosen People came out of Egypt, free from subjection to its laws and culture, able to reveal to the world the radical freedom of those who know the One Commandment:

> Hear, O Israel: The LORD is our God, the LORD alone. You shall love the LORD your God with *all* your heart, and with *all* your soul, and with *all* your might.

Him only shall you fear; him only shall you serve. "Do not follow any of the gods of the peoples around you."[5]

Like Israel, we who passed through the water of Baptism have "come out of Egypt," freed from slavery to any authority but God's. We obey human laws with the "freedom of the children of God, in "singleness of heart," with undivided loyalty to God, obeying humans, not "in order to please

them, but as slaves of Christ, doing the will of God from the heart."[6]

To accept this freedom is to renounce slavery to our culture. We don't conform to what is expected in our society. We don't "follow any of the gods of the people around us." We don't assume their attitudes. We don't embrace their values. We are different. In Baptism we were consecrated as *prophets*, "anointed" with the "power of the Spirit."

> *This is the night when Jesus Christ broke the chains of death and rose triumphant from the grave.*

To be a "prophet" is to profess the faith through a lifestyle that doesn't make sense without it: one that cannot be explained except through the Light and Life of the risen Jesus present and active within us, sweeping aside darkness and fear of death. This is the core of Christian *witness*.

POSTERITY

> *This is our Passover feast, when Christ, the true Lamb is slain whose blood consecrates the homes of all believers....*

We are sanctified as a community. It is not just our hearts, but our homes that are consecrated.

> *Christians everywhere... are restored to grace and grow together in holiness.*

Christianity is a communal experience:

> They devoted themselves to the apostles' teaching and fellowship, to the breaking of bread and the prayers.... Day by day, as they spent much time together in the temple, they broke bread at home and ate their food with glad and generous hearts, praising God....[7]

The mystery of our baptismal anointing as *priests in the Priest* consecrates and commits us to be *priests* to one another, to minister to each other at home and in church as family. And promises us a *posterity*. Our lives will be fruitful in divine life for others.

As children of the Father, "from whom every family in heaven and on earth takes its name," we are fathers and mothers, brothers and sisters to one another in the "family of believers." We help all to grow in love for the Father, in union with the Son, through the gifts of the Spirit given to all for the good of all:

> To each is given the manifestation of the Spirit for the common good.… to equip the saints for the work of *ministry*, for building up the body of Christ,
>
> We must grow up in every way into him who is the head, into Christ, from whom the whole body, joined and knit together… as each part is working properly, *promotes the body's growth in building itself up in love.*[8]

VICTORY

We are sent, not just to one another, but to extend the family of God until it embraces the whole human race. Jesus came to establish the "reign of God" on earth; to draw all of humanity into the "peace and unity of his kingdom." And he has entrusted this task to us. This is the "mystery of meaningfulness" that transforms, redirects, and enhances the value of all our human labor in the world. By our baptismal consecration as "kings" we were appointed and empowered by God to establish the reign of his love over every area and activity of human life on earth. And we were promised *victory*.

> The power of this holy night dispels all evil… brings mourners joy. It casts out

> hatred, brings us peace and humbles earthly pride.
>
> Night truly blessed, when heaven is wedded to earth and humans are reconciled with God.

This is the image of the "wedding banquet of the Lamb," where all will be celebrating together, in perfect union with each other and with God. All offenses forgotten in unrestricted forgiveness; all differences and divisions overcome in total reconciliation. This is the "Kingdom of God." In God's time it is already established. In our time we are committed and empowered to persevere in faith and fidelity, working as "*stewards* of his kingship" until Christ comes again in triumph.

WE HAVE "BECOME CHRIST"

All is included in the central mystery of "the grace of the Lord Jesus Christ," the favor of sharing in the divine life of God. We have "*become Christ*," committed to let him live and act *with* us, *in* us, and *through* us to "save" everything we are involved in. This commits us to seek ongoing enlightenment through *discipleship*, and to embrace his mission as *prophets*, *priests*, and *stewards* of his kingship.

That is the mystery and promise of Easter, the call and commitment we exult in.

[1]*John* 1:4, 8:11; *Psalms* 36:9; 56:13; *Proverbs* 6:23; *Matthew* 11:25-30.
[2]See *Isaiah* 11:2-3; *Galatians* 5:22-23.
[3]*2Corinthians* 5:21.
[4]*John* 8:31-32.
[5]*Deuteronomy* 6:4-14.
[6]*Romans* 8:15-27; *Ephesians* 6:5-6.
[7]*Acts* 2:42-46.
[8]*John* 15:16; *1Corinthians* 4:14-15; 12:1-27; *Ephesians* 3:14-15; 4:11-16; *1Peter* 2:17; *Galatians* 4:19.

Initiative: Renew your Baptismal promises during the Easter Vigil as a *conscious commitment* to live out in joy the five mysteries and commitments of your Baptism.

APRIL 24, 2011

To remember is to *re-member* ourselves: to re-commit as members of Christ's risen body on earth.

INVENTORY

On a day-to-day basis, how conscious are you of your Baptism? If you were asked to name your baptismal commitments right now, could you do it?

What do you think about at Mass during the *Presentation of Gifts*?

INPUT

The *Entrance Antiphon* begins with words inspired by *Psalm* 139, verse 18: The psalmist says, "I have risen: I am with you once more...." We need to be constantly "rising" or "waking up" to be with God "once more." Physical life is a process of constant renewal, and so is spiritual life. So on Easter Sunday we have the *Renewal of Baptismal Promises*, "when we rejected Satan and his works and promised to serve God faithfully" as *Christians, Disciples, Prophets, Priests*, and *Stewards of his Kingship*. We renew the promises to remind us of our commitment. This stimulates us to live it out more consciously. The *Instruction* provides that "on Sundays, especially in Easter time, in place of the customary *Penitential Rite*, the blessing and sprinkling with water may occasionally be performed to recall Baptism."

The *Opening Prayer*(s) repeat this theme: we ask God to "raise us up and renew our lives" by the Spirit given to us at Baptism. And remembering that after his resurrection "the Lord appeared to men who had begun to lose hope," we ask him to renew our hope through the Mass: "May the risen Lord breathe on our minds and open our eyes, that we may know him in the breaking of the bread." The goal is a renewal of commitment to "follow him in his risen life."

In the *Prayer over the Gifts* we call Eucharist "the sacrifice by which your Church is reborn and nourished." At every Mass we are invited to stand up, reborn out of Baptism's grave, and say to God: "I have risen: I am with you once more...." It is a time to *remember and re-commit*, as a "new creation," to let the Christ whose body we have become live and act *with* us, *in* us, and *through* us in everything we do.

THE CALL TO WITNESS

In his initial explanation of the Good News to the Gentiles, **Acts 10:34-43**, Peter uses the word "witness" three times: "*We are witnesses* of all that [Jesus of Nazareth] did.... *witnesses* chosen beforehand by God... commissioned to bear *witness* that he is the one...." Obviously, Peter could not think of the Good News or of himself without awareness of his call to bear witness—a call that belongs to all of us through our baptismal anointing as *prophets*.

The liturgy invites us to make Peter's attitude toward this call our own. We embrace it in the *Responsorial* (*Psalm* 118):

8

"This is the day the Lord has made; let us rejoice and be glad."

"GONE AHEAD OF YOU"

Matthew 28:1-10 begins: "As the first day of the week was dawning...." This is the dawn of Christianity. A new beginning. In daylight, when people go to work.

Christ is risen. The seekers are told that if they want to see him, they have to get moving! The angel told the women at the tomb, "He is not here. He *goes ahead of you* to Galilee. There you will see him." Jesus repeated the same message: "Go and carry the news to my brothers that *they are to go* to Galilee. There they will see me."

Galilee here is synonymous with mission. "Most of the events of the Synoptic Gospels occurred in Galilee, and there Jesus spent most of his life and most of his ministry."[1] If we want to "see" Jesus, we will find him by joining him in his mission.

To commit to the mission of the Messiah is a mystical experience. It is the experience of call, of being personally invited and empowered by God to do the work of Jesus. Until we hear this call, until we feel moved to take on the work of the Church, we are still "infants" in the faith. Children's only duty is to develop themselves and grow to maturity. But the mark of maturity is to go beyond oneself in dedication to work that contributes to the well-being of others. We are adults in the Church when we take on the work of the Church.[2]

People sometimes say they don't find Mass "meaningful." The short answer to this is to paraphrase St. John of the Cross and say, "Where you don't find meaning, put meaning and you will find it." But what does "meaning" mean?

A dictionary definition is: "adding significance or purpose to somebody's life."[3] The Mass explicitly does this.

During the *Presentation of Gifts*, we are called to "present our bodies as a living sacrifice to God" in reaffirmation of our Baptism. We send up, as a symbol of ourselves, a host to be placed on the altar, lose its existence as bread, be transformed and offered as the body of Christ for the life of the world. This is without doubt an act that "adds significance, meaning and purpose" to our lives. If we mean it.

But if we don't pay attention to what is happening or to what we are doing, but just sing the hymn along with the choir or watch the altar servers preparing the altar, we won't experience anything very meaningful. For that we have to consciously be aware of what the *Presentation of Gifts* is expressing at that moment, make it our own expression, and mean what we express.

What we are expressing is dedication to mission. We are reaffirming our Baptism, declaring our deliberate participation in all that the Mass means and expresses, and presenting ourselves under the form of the bread and wine to be offered with Christ for the life of the world.

> May the Lord *accept the sacrifice...* for our good and that of *all his Church.*

"A FRESH DOUGH"

1Corinthians 5:6-8 invites us to see the bread being carried up to the altar as us.

Paul tells us to be a "fresh dough." To bring a prophetic freshness to the Church and to the world. To live in a way that makes it obvious Christianity, our religion, is not just the "same old same old." This is what it means to bear *witness* to the risen, the living Jesus, the Jesus present and acting in us who are his real body on earth. Now.

To do this, Paul says we have to "get rid of the old yeast." What is that?

Yeast is the moving factor. It is what makes the dough rise to become bread. In us, and in human society, the "yeast" is what makes us "rise to the bait" when something is held up before us as an object of choice. The yeast is that complex of attitudes, values, desires, compulsions, fears, and expectations that are the interior make-up of each one of us. The yeast is everything prior to free choice itself, but which has the greatest influence on what our free choices will be. The yeast determines the "chronic priorities," recognized or not, that we bring to every encounter with every object of choice. Whether what is offered is good or bad, the yeast is what makes us spontaneously rise to the bait or be unresponsive to it. It takes an act of free will to actually get hooked on what expands or diminishes life, but the yeast determines the attraction.

The "old yeast" is cultural conditioning. It is made up of all the attitudes, values, etc. that have been "programmed" into us since our first contact with the human race in a society corrupted, as all societies are, by many false attitudes, values, and patterns of behavior. To "get rid of the old yeast" is to declare oneself free—and prove it by living by Christ's standards instead of by those of the culture.

The *Presentation of Gifts* reminds us at every Mass to be "fresh dough." But we need to put ourselves consciously on the paten to be presented, transformed, offered, and shared as the "unleavened bread of sincerity and truth."

"Of sincerity": not corrupted, not ruled by the shortsighted standards of the "world" or the blind impulses of the "flesh." And "of truth": not the truth of this world's orbit, but the Truth of the Way that is divine and the Life that is proper to God.

Every time we do this, "the first day of the week is dawning." It is a new day, a new beginning, a new hope for humanity. *"This is the day the Lord has made; let us rejoice and be glad."*

[1]McKenzie, *Dictionary of the Bible*, under "Galilee."
[2]This is the context in which Paul wrote his famous "Hymn to love" in *1Corinthians*, chapters 13-14. He is telling the Corinthians to "grow up" by dedicating themselves to "building up" the Church.
[3]Encarta® World English Dictionary © 1999 Microsoft Corporation.

INSIGHT
Do I find new meaning now in the Presentation of Gifts?

INITIATIVE
Make the Presentation of Gifts a moment of intense personal recommitment.

April 25, 2011

The *Responsorial* (*Psalm* 16) begins: "*Keep me safe, O God, you are my hope.*" The rest of the Psalm shows that the "hope" is really for immortality.

As interpreted by Peter in **Acts 2:14-33**, David "foresaw and spoke of the resurrection of the Messiah." Peter says God freed Jesus from the grip of death because "it was impossible that death should keep its hold on him." The reading ends with Peter declaring: "of this we are all witnesses."

In the following verses (33-35), he tells why it was "impossible" for Jesus to be held by death. In contrast to David, who "died and was buried, and his grave is with us to this day," Jesus was not just human; he was divine. Jesus is God the Son, "exalted at the right hand of the Father." Together with the Father he "poured forth the Holy Spirit" at Pentecost. Christ changed everything for us, because by Baptism we too were made divine. Through incorporation into his body we "became Christ," true children of the Father, our bodies the dwelling place of the Holy Spirit.

When Christ died, he not only died for all, but all died in him. Taking us and our sins into his body, Jesus was "made to be sin... so that in him we might become the righteousness of God."[1] As a "new creation," each of us can say the words of the Psalm with Jesus, "You will not abandon my soul to the nether world, or let your holy one experience corruption," at least, not a disintegration of the body that endures. Our bodies too will rise again. It is impossible that they should not. We are divine.[2]

The presider's prayer over the bread and wine during the *Presentation of Gifts* emphasizes the transformation from human to divine that is at the core of Christianity. "We have this bread to offer, which *earth has given* and *human* hands have made. It will become for us the *bread of life.*" It reminds us that we who "eat this bread," though formed from the "clay of the ground" and destined to "return to the ground from which we were taken," have now "put on immortality," because we have "put on the Lord Jesus Christ."

> The first man was from the earth, a man of dust; the second man is from heaven.... Just as we have borne the image of the man of dust, we will also bear the image of the man of heaven.

We are aware that the bread we see is about to become what we do not see: the "Bread of life." It reminds us we are called to make his invisible, divine life in us visible in behavior inexplicable without it. This is *witness.*[3]

Matthew 28:8-15 reminds us that we must "not be afraid," but "go and carry the Good News" as "witnesses to all the world of what we have seen and heard."[4] What we see at Mass, what we hear in the *Liturgy of the Word*, is not to lie dormant in us. We need to contradict the "story that circulates" in our culture.

[1] Or "the very holiness" (1970 *New American Bible*).
[2] *2Corinthians* 5:1-21.
[3] *Genesis* 2:7; 3:19; *Romans* 13:14; *1Corinthians* 15:35-57; *John* 6:48-51; 20:26-29. And see *Eucharistic Prayer IV.*
[4] See *Acts* 22:15.

Decision: At the *Presentation of Gifts* look and listen. See yourself in the bread.

11

APRIL 26, 2011

The *Responsorial* (*Psalm* 33) proclaims: "*The earth is full of the goodness of the Lord.*" But not completely! In **Acts 2:36-41** Peter exhorts the people, "Save yourselves from this generation which has gone astray."

There is a negative as well as a positive meaning in the presider's words during the *Presentation of Gifts*. Like the bread and wine, the human nature we present to God is something "earth has given." God created us from the "clay of the ground" and created us good. "God looked at everything he had made and he found it very good."[1]

But not for long. God made humans free. God created our human nature, and it is good. But as *persons* we are something "human hands have made." Our choices form us and make us what we are as persons. We can choose to be good or bad.

Never totally, of course.

> There is so much good in the worst of us
> And so much bad in the best of us,
> That it ill behooves the rest of us
> To criticize what's left of us.

Still, we do make bad choices. And every choice, good or bad, not only has an effect on us; it also puts something into the environment that never goes away. The attitudes and values we express influence others. Expressed often enough, they tend to become characteristic of a culture. Then everyone born into that culture is influenced by them—even before becoming old enough to make a free choice. Our society can "program" us to think and act spontaneously in ways we have never consciously considered or chosen. We call this "cultural conditioning." This is what Peter is talking about when he urges, "Save yourselves from this generation which has gone astray."

The task of the *prophets* is to challenge the culture through a lifestyle so different that they "radiate faith in values that go beyond current values, and hope in something not seen.... Through this wordless witness they stir up irresistible questions in the hearts of those who see how they live: Why are they like this?"[2]

To be consecrated to this, Peter says, "you must reform, and be baptized... then you will receive the *gift of the Holy Spirit*." The gift of the prophets.

John 20:11-18 begins with Mary weeping and ends with her proclaiming, "I have seen the Lord." The core of all witness is personal encounter with the living Jesus. Everything else comes from that. Once we know him, we are driven to know him better through the study of his mind and heart as revealed in the word of God. We become *disciples*. Then, as we take on his mission as *prophets, priests,* and *stewards of his Kingship*, we reverse the darkness and death of "this generation that has gone astray" until "*the earth is full of the goodness of the Lord.*" This is a motive to "present our bodies" again at the *Presentation of Gifts*.

[1]*Genesis* 1:24-31; 2:7.
[2]Paul VI, *Evangelization in the Modern World*, no. 21.

Decision: Save yourself and others from the infection of the culture. Be a prophet.

April 27, 2011

The *Responsorial* (*Psalm* 105) gives us the key to joy: "*Rejoice, O hearts that seek the Lord.*" It is as simple as that.

The man in **Acts 3:1-10** had been "crippled from birth." He wasn't particularly happy with it, but he was resigned. He wasn't even seeking a cure: just alms.

If we are honest, we have to admit many Christians are "crippled from birth" in the way they live their religion. It isn't that they are committing great sins (that they recognize, at least). It is just that they seem to be going nowhere. Or barely limping along. And they don't enjoy the journey. It's okay; it's just not exciting. They do what they "have to do," and accept with resignation that this is what religion is.

Except for the younger ones. They just stop going to church because they "get nothing out of it."

Everything changed for the lame man when he met Jesus—not Jesus in his earthly life, but the risen Jesus. Peter said to him, "Look at us." There was something about Peter and John that was different. He didn't know what it was, but it was enough that "he paid attention to them, expecting to receive something from them."

If we are *witnesses* to the risen Christ by a lifestyle so different it cannot be explained except by his life within us, people will begin to "pay attention" to the phenomenon of the community that believes. They will begin to analyze the example of the believers they live and work with. If they come to Mass, it

will be with a different attitude, "expecting to receive something." They will listen to the readings with a questioning mind. Why? Because they will see that those who are "witnesses" have something they want.

The turned-off and tepid can be turned on and fired up. Those who experience "religion" as an unexciting system of doctrines, rules, and observances will discover the "spirituality" of the life of grace: dynamic, exciting, personal interaction with God as Father, Son, and Spirit. Life "in the grace lane" is living on the level of God. It is an ongoing mystical experience. The key is in what we are looking for: "Rejoice, O hearts that *seek the Lord.*" Do we want to encounter the living Jesus? Do we interact with him in everything we do?

Luke 24:13-35 parallels the Mass. Jesus' questions, like the *Introductory Rites*, focus us on what the Good News is supposed to be. Then, as in the *Liturgy of the Word*, he "interpreted the Scriptures" to them. But the real encounter came in the "breaking of the bread," the *Liturgy of the Eucharist*.

If, during the *Presentation of Gifts* we consciously reaffirm our Baptism, send ourselves up intentionally under the sign of bread to be placed on the altar, and ask intensely for ongoing transformation—"Father, bring the image of your Son to perfection within us"—our "eyes will be opened." We will realize "our hearts were burning within us" during the Scripture readings and that he "was made known to us in the breaking of the bread." But only those who look will find: "*Rejoice, O hearts that seek the Lord.*"

Decision: Where you don't find meaning, put meaning by interacting with Jesus.

13

April 28, 2011

The *Responsorial* (*Psalm* 8) is a prayer of praise and thanksgiving for the gift of creation, and especially for the dignity God has given to the human race: *"O Lord, our God, how wonderful your name in all the earth!"*

> When I look at your heavens, the work of your fingers, the moon and the stars that you have established; what are humans that you are mindful of them, or the children of men that you care for them?

The presider echoes this praise of God as Creator when he prays over the bread and wine: "Blessed are you, Lord, God of all creation, through your goodness we have this bread to offer." But then the prayer takes us into a whole new dimension of God's goodness: "It will become for us the Bread of life."

God is not just Creator, giving us human life as "children of men." He is the Redeemer and Sanctifier who shares with us his own divine life, making us children of God. The "bread of the children" he gives us becomes the Bread of Life (*John* 6:30-59).

Matthew uses the word "bread" (*artos*) to tie together the passages he wrote on the multiplication of the loaves (15:26, 32-39), the Pharisees' insistence on a "sign from heaven" (16:1-4), and Jesus' reproach to his disciples for not recognizing him as the kind of Messiah he really came to be (16:5-12), which was the secret they were about to reject when he revealed it (16:21-28).

Jesus warned his disciples against the "yeast of the Pharisees" who expected a Messiah who would use divine power to give people human satisfaction on earth. This was Jesus' first temptation in the desert (4:3): to change stones to bread as a sign that he brought prosperity. But even after the two "bread signs" (16:9-10), the disciples did not understand the difference between a Messiah who gives the bread of human life and one who gives the Bread of divine life.

The *Presentation of Gifts* invites us to reaffirm our faith in the central mystery of our redemption: the linking of human and divine. God "humbled himself to share in our humanity" so that he might die and rise as the Bread of Life, making us "sharers in his divinity."

Peter is preaching this in **Acts 3:11-26:** "The God of our fathers has glorified his servant Jesus... the author of life [whom] you put to death." It is "faith in his name," the crucified and risen, that gives "fulfillment," "perfect health," and the "restoration of all things."

We place ourselves on the altar with the bread and wine to be offered with Christ and in Christ, reaffirming our Baptism into his death and resurrection. And we echo the presider's prayer: "Blessed be God forever." *"O Lord, our God, how wonderful your name in all the earth!"*

Luke 24:35-48 ends with Jesus saying, "You are witnesses of these things." We are the "prophets of the Prophet," sent to proclaim the transformation of bread into Bread, of the human into the divine, of life into Life, and of death into Life everlasting. We know the Good News. We celebrate it in Eucharist. Our lifestyle should cry out, *"O Lord, our God, how wonderful your name in all the earth!"*

Decision: Be a prophet. Live in a way that proclaims life through death.

APRIL 29, 2011

What is the difference between the offering we put in the collection basket and the symbolic gesture of sending up a host that represents us to be placed on the altar?

For one, the money we give is not a symbol of our whole selves, but of our labor: of whatever we did to earn it. And it is not transformed into the body of Christ offered for the salvation of the world, but is simply a contribution to the particular ministries Jesus is doing through a parish: the members of his body on earth today gathered together as a recognized community and acting officially in the name of the Church.

More important: we assign to the collection only part of the money we are managing for God as his *stewards*. But the host stands for our whole selves. In sending it up to be placed on the altar we are giving all that we are.

That is why Peter says in **Acts 4:1-12,** "There is salvation in no one else, for there is no other name under heaven given among mortals by which we must be saved." Jesus is not one aid to salvation among others, with devotion to him a contributing factor. Jesus *is* salvation. He and he alone is the "Bread of Life." We don't invest part of our resources to buy a part interest in Jesus. For Jesus we give all for All. And we express it by sending up a host that represents us to be placed on the altar and lose its existence. The bread ceases to exist as bread. It becomes the Body of Christ existing as God by God's own act of existing. In a similar way, by Baptism we give up our human lives in

order to rise out of the waters a "new creation," existing still as human, but totally committed to living by the divine life of God. In Baptism we "lose our life to find it." We give up our lives as isolated human individuals in order to share communally in the divine life of Jesus as members of his body. We are like grains of wheat that have given up being isolated grains in order to become one bread. Branches on the vine. The vine apart from whom we can "do nothing."[1]

That is why the *Presentation of Gifts* is such an intense moment of the Mass. In one symbolic gesture we are reaffirming and reliving our Baptism, the death and resurrection of Jesus, and our acceptance of communal, relational existence in the Church.

The *Responsorial* (*Psalm* 118) tells us Jesus was *"the stone rejected by the builders"* because the power structure of Israel—the priests, Sadducees, "rulers, elders, and scribes"—were not willing to die to the sense of control they had over their earthbound existence and "lose themselves" in the mystery of divine life "in Christ." But for us he *"has become the cornerstone."* In the *Presentation of Gifts* we are saying this.

John 21:1-14: Jesus again previews Eucharist. Before feeding his disciples he calls them to "present" the fish they had caught. We present the "work of human hands" at the *Presentation of Gifts* and receive back the Bread of Life. Jesus makes human efforts bear divine fruit. The theme song of redemption!

[1] 2Corinthians 5:14-17; *John* 12:23-25; 15:5.

Decision: Enter into mystery at the *Presentation of Gifts.* Give all for All.

APRIL 30, 2011

The *Responsorial* (*Psalm* 118) gives credit to God for the prophets' courage in bearing witness and for the faith of those who receive it: "*I will give thanks to you, for you have answered me.*"

Jesus could not have found anything more ordinary to turn into his Body and Blood than what we put on the altar during the *Presentation of Gifts*. Bread and wine were the commonplace food of his time. Not anything precious, rare, or exotic to set people up to believe in mystery. In the Eucharist God is made present under appearances that are about as ordinary as you can get. And it is in and through the most ordinary, unimpressive people that he continues to reveal his presence on earth today. In us.

We may be impressive in all sorts of ways according to the standards of our society: rich, successful, recognized, honored, and famous. But when we put ourselves on the altar during the *Presentation of Gifts*, it is under the simple appearances of bread and wine. Think about that.

Acts 4:13-21 shows us the "leaders, elders, and scribes" rejecting the witness of Peter and John because they were "uneducated, ordinary men." The Greek words are *agrammatoi* "illiterate or uneducated," and *idiotai*, for which the first meaning is "laymen"; that is, not experts of any kind. They "recognized them" only as "companions of Jesus" and were not impressed.[1]

But before we get too judgmental, we should note that in **Mark 16:9-15** those same "companions"—all eleven of what we would call the original "college of bishops"—rejected the eyewitness testimony of Mary Magdalen and of the men who met Jesus on the road to Emmaus. And Jesus "rebuked them for their unbelief and hardness of heart, because they had not believed those who saw him after he had been raised." The Christian "leaders and elders" were no more open to the testimony of the "uneducated ordinary laity" than the Jewish leaders were. Prejudice is prejudice, and common to us all, no matter what our religion is or our position in it.

Knowing the prejudice (and worse) that his followers would meet, Jesus still sent them: "Go into the whole world and proclaim the Gospel to every creature." And he told them what to expect:

> If you belonged to the world, the world would love you as its own. Because... I have chosen you out of the world—therefore the world hates you.

The prophets will encounter the "world" and its spirit both inside and outside the Church. Vatican II was clear about this:

> The Church, embracing sinners in its bosom [among clergy and laity alike], is at the same time holy and always in need of being purified, and incessantly pursues the path of penance [*metanoia*, "change of mind and heart"] and renewal.[2]

Every one of us is called to contribute to that renewal in every age—with trust in God: "*I will give thanks to you, for you have answered me.*" That is why we put ourselves on the altar.

[1] Bauer's *Greek-English Lexicon of the New Testament*, Univ. of Chicago, 1979.
[2] *John* 15:16-20. See Vatican II, "The Church," nos. 8, 33, 51.

Decision: Be humbled as bread, but exalted as a witness to the Bread of Life.

FOR REFLECTION AND DISCUSSION: EASTER WEEK ONE

During the *Presentation of Gifts* we send up, as a symbol of ourselves, a host to be placed on the altar, lose its existence as bread, be transformed and offered as the body of Christ for the life of the world. This is an act that adds significance, meaning, and purpose to our lives.

Invitation:

Make the *Presentation of Gifts* a moment of intense personal recommitment.

Ask yourself in prayer and others in discussion: How could the statements below make Mass mean more if we stay aware of them during Mass?

Acts 2:14-33: The *Presentation of Gifts* emphasizes the transformation from human to divine that is at the core of Christianity. "We have this bread... which *earth has given* and *human* hands have made. It will become... the *bread of life*."

We who share his divine life are called to live "no longer for ourselves, but for him": to live as he did, to give "our flesh for the life of the world."

Acts 2:36-41: Like the bread and wine, the human nature we present to God is something "earth has given." It is good. But as *persons* we are something "human hands have made." We can choose to be good or bad.

The task of the *prophets* is to challenge the culture through a different lifestyle.

Acts 3:1-10: If we are *witnesses* to the risen Jesus by a lifestyle so different it cannot be explained except by his life within us, people will begin to "pay attention" to the phenomenon of the community that believes.

The turned-off and tepid can be turned on and fired up. Those who experience "religion" as an unexciting system of doctrines, rules, and observances can discover the "spirituality" of dynamic, exciting, personal interaction with God.

Acts 3:11-26: The *Presentation of Gifts* invites us to reaffirm our faith in the central mystery of our redemption: God "humbled himself to share in our humanity" and died to rise as the Bread of Life, making us "sharers in his divinity."

Acts 4:1-12: Jesus alone is the "Bread of Life." For Jesus we give all for All. And we express it by sending up a host that represents us to be placed on the altar and lose its existence. In Baptism we "die" with Christ to "rise" as his body on earth.

In Baptism and Mass we give up our lives as isolated "grains of wheat" in order to live communally by the divine life of Jesus as "one bread," members of his body.

Acts 4:13-21: We put ourselves on the altar during the *Presentation of Gifts* as very ordinary people, under the simple appearances of bread and wine. But we bear witness to the divine life we have "in Christ," the Bread of Life.

Decisions:

At the Presentation of Gifts look and listen. See yourself in the bread.
Where you don't find meaning during Mass, put meaning by offering yourself.
Enter into mystery at the *Presentation of Gifts*. Give all for All.

MAY 1, 2011

And Divine Mercy Sunday
Experiencing and Expressing the Risen Life

INVENTORY

When do you experience yourself as most alive by grace? How much of it depends on what you yourself are doing? How much on what other people are doing (or doing together with you)?

INPUT

The *Opening Prayer* reminds us that we must "no longer look for Jesus among the dead"—including the deadening routine of just "saying prayers" or participating in Mass without attention—for "he has become the Lord of *life*." We ask God to "increase in our minds and hearts [our experience of] the *risen life* we *share with Christ*." This will "help us to *grow*... toward the *fullness* of eternal life." We are asking for a religion brought alive by the *experience* of life—of Christ's life within us.

The *Readings* show us how we become aware of this experience. The *Responsorial* (*Psalm* 118) puts into words the spontaneous response it evokes: *"Give thanks to the Lord for he is good, his love is everlasting."*

AN AWESOME EXPERIENCE:

Acts 2:42-47 describes the experience of the first people who responded with faith to the Apostles' proclamation of the Good News: "They *devoted themselves* to the *teaching* of the Apostles, and to the *communal life*, to the breaking of the bread and to the prayers." The result of this was *"exultation* and sincerity of heart." And: "Every day the Lord *added to their number* those who were being saved."

What we have here is a formula for experiencing the risen life. The first two elements are *discipleship*—a real desire and commitment to *learn* everything Jesus taught—and *community*—a commitment to gathering and celebrating the Good News with others.

The next line gives us the third element: "All who believed... would *sell their property* and possessions and divide them among all according to each one's need." This, more than any miracles, was the greatest "wonder and sign" brought about by the Apostles' preaching. This was the "sign of Jonah," the visible evidence of the risen Jesus alive and active in the hearts of the community. To reveal (to ourselves as well as others) that we are alive by grace, we don't have to literally sell our possessions. But we do have to give up selfishness and all selfish attachment to what we own, and respond to the needs of others with the same love Jesus shows to us. When we see others doing this, and experience ourselves doing it also, that is when the life of grace becomes for us an awesome experience. Then

18

we have something deep and personal to celebrate. *"Give thanks to the Lord for he is good, his love is everlasting."*

When the fruit of grace, the fruit of Christ's divine life within us, is *visible in our actions*, that is when we are bearing *witness* as *prophets*.

HOW DO WE KNOW…?

How do we know we are alive by grace and sharing in Christ's own divine life? **1Peter 1:3-9** tells us we know it when we see ourselves living in a way that cannot be explained without it.

This letter was written to Christians facing persecution. It tells them that their fear itself is an experience of their faith, because in spite of it they are remaining faithful.

> You rejoice, even if now for a little while you have had to suffer various trials, so that the genuineness of your faith… tested by fire… may be found to result in praise and glory and honor when Jesus Christ is revealed.

To our human way of perceiving things, the visible threat of death is a lot more real than the invisible promise of eternal life. But the point of the letter is that if we choose to remain faithful, *the experience of believing is just as real as the experience of fearing death*. We experience the promise of eternal life, not just as words of Jesus handed down to us, but as words Jesus is speaking now in our own hearts.

How do we know he is speaking? We know it because we have enough certitude in faith to die for the sake of the promise. The deep certitude we experience (without necessarily *feeling* it)

cannot be explained except by the divine gift of faith. We know that we know. And we know that nothing human can explain the fact that we know. Our willingness to die requires as the "condition for its possibility" the reality of our faith in Christ's promise. That is when we know our faith is real. As Karl Rahner has said, "We do not know we believe in the two birds in the bush until we *let go* of the one bird in our hand."

Peter's letter makes the point: "Even though you do not see him now, you believe in him and rejoice… for you are receiving [and experiencing] the *outcome of your faith*, the salvation of your souls." By his fruits in our heart we know him.

So we know that we are sharing in Christ's divine life when we find ourselves *acting* in a way that can only be explained by divine faith, hope, and love. We do not have to face death for this. We experience it whenever we let go of any "bird in the hand" for the sake of what is promised by the Voice in the burning bush. This is the role and the experience of the *prophets*, who live in counter-cultural ways inspired by the voice of God in their hearts. When we go beyond "what everybody does," we know our faith is personal—that we ourselves are listening and responding to the living God. Then we can personally *"give thanks to the Lord,"* for we ourselves know that *"he is good, his love is everlasting."*

UNLESS I SEE AND TOUCH…

When the risen Jesus appears to his disciples in **John 20:19-31** his opening word is always, "Peace…." Where does that peace come from?

Jesus' first words after the greeting tell us. The first time, "When he had said this, he *showed them his hands and his side*." He showed them the proof of his passion and death so they would know that the living man in front of them had truly risen from the dead. The first source of our peace is in the fact that Jesus is risen and living still. Still with us.

After his second greeting, Jesus said, "As the Father has sent me, so I send you." Then he "breathed on them and said, "Receive the Holy Spirit." The second source of our peace is in the fact that we are *sent and empowered* by the Spirit to continue Christ's work on earth. We have a meaning and purpose in life. We know what we are here for and what we have to do. And we know that the light and strength to do it are coming, not from us, but from the gift of the Spirit within us. In other words, we know that the risen Jesus is living and acting in us.

Jesus said he would go down into the grave to rise multiplied through res-urrection in every living member of his body on earth: "Unless a grain of wheat falls into the earth and dies, it remains just a single grain; but if it dies, it bears much fruit" (*John* 12:24). Our peace is in the fact that Jesus is risen and living in us.

But Thomas could not find this peace just from the other disciples' report that they had seen Jesus. He said, "Unless I see the mark of the nails in his hands and touch his wounds myself, "I will not believe."

Thank God for hard-headed disciples! Thomas voiced the need we all have to see flesh-and-blood evidence that Jesus is risen and real. And we find it in the flesh-and-blood reality of his body on earth, in the flesh-and-blood experience that we and others are living the divine life of Jesus risen and living in us. Every time we act in a way that nothing but faith can explain, Jesus in us is saying to anyone who doubts, "See my hands. Touch me. And do not be unbelieving but believe—that through this belief you may have *life*."

INSIGHT
What do I do that cannot be explained except by my faith in Jesus Christ? Are there things I do that I know I would not do unless I was motivated by faith, even though other people might do them for other motives?

INITIATIVE
Take God's words seriously. Make some choices consciously based on them.

MAY 2, 2011

The *Responsorial* (*Psalm* 2) reminds us where power and security lie: "*Happy are all who take refuge in the Lord.*"

In **Acts 4:23-31** Peter and John report to the community that they have been commanded by the priests and elders "not to speak or teach at all in the name of Jesus." The response of the community is to quote Psalm 2: "Why did the Gentiles rage, and the peoples imagine vain things... against the Lord and against his Messiah?"

They are grounding their life and action in the most basic truth perceived by human intelligence: that nothing exists except by God's ongoing will to continue his creative act. We *are* only because God is saying "*Beeeee...*" And prolonging the creative command. We can *move* and act only because God within us is empowering us to convert our existence into action.

The philosophers call our existence "first act" and our operations "second act"—not because they are two separate acts of God, but because *existence* is God's actualization of the power he has to make nothingness exist as a being, and *operation* is God's concurrence in a being's actualization of the power it has to use existence according to its nature. Paul put this on the table when the "Epicurean and Stoic philosophers debated with him" in Athens: "I proclaim to you the God who made the world and everything in it, he who is Lord of heaven and earth.... since he himself gives to all mortals life and breath and all things....

For 'In him we live and move and have our being.'"[1]

This is the recognition every human choice should be based on. We acknowledge it at every Mass in the *Presentation of Gifts*: "Blessed are you, Lord, God of all creation. Through your goodness we have...." Forget that, and every choice we make is baseless. Remember that, and we are grounded in truth and security: "*Happy are all who take refuge in the Lord.*"

But God goes beyond giving us existence. In **John 3:1-8** Jesus tells Nicodemus that we need to receive life on a higher level by being "born from above... of water and Spirit." We say in the *Presentation of Gifts* that this bread "which earth has given and human hands have made" will become "the bread of life." Likewise, this human life which God gave when he "formed us from the dust of the ground, and breathed into us the breath of life" is meant to become eternal life, divine life, a sharing in the Life of God himself.[2]

In every Mass we are reminded of this. In every Mass we need to reaffirm our faith that this mystery is true, our hope that its promise will be fully realized in us, our love for God giving us life that is both human and divine. We do this by "presenting our bodies" under the form of bread to be offered as a "living sacrifice" to God as we did on the day of Baptism: "May the Lord accept the sacrifice at your hands...."[3]

[1] *Acts* 17:16-29.
[2] *Genesis* 2:7.
[3] *Romans* 12:1.

Decision: Recognize God as Creator by intelligence and as Father by faith.

MAY 3, 2011

Feast of Saints Philip and James, Apostles[1]

The *Responsorial* (*Psalm* 19) predicts: *"Their message goes out to all the earth."* But how do we present it?

We tell children, as Ananias told Paul, that sins are "washed away" in Baptism. Not a threatening image. But is it possible to explain how Baptism takes away sin without speaking of death?

In **1Corinthians 15:1-8** Paul says *"Christ died for our sins… was buried, and raised…"* Peter also says, "Christ *'suffered for'* our sins…" There is nothing threatening about Christ suffering and dying for us. That is extrinsic to us. But when Paul explains the mystery more deeply, he says that in "Baptism *we ourselves* have to die."

> All of us who have been baptized into Christ Jesus were baptized into his death. Therefore we have been buried with him by baptism into death, so that, just as Christ was raised from the dead… we too might walk in newness of life.

Paul says our "old self *was crucified with him* so that the body of sin might be *destroyed…* For whoever *has died* is freed from sin."[2]

We usually don't tell children that in Baptism we ourselves have to die. We take the mystery out of Baptism. This makes "walk in newness of life" just an exhortation to good human behavior. It also leaves us with the impression our sins were only "forgiven," not "taken away." Being forgiven does not change us; dying and rising again does.

This "dumbs down" the whole mystery of Christian identity. We miss the reality of Paul's conclusions: "In the one Spirit we were all *baptized into one body*—Jews or Greeks, slaves or free" and "As many of you as were baptized *into Christ* have *clothed yourselves with Christ*." These are intrinsic changes in us that no extrinsic "payment for sin" can produce. It is only because *we died* in Christ and rose in him that Paul can say, "From now on, therefore, we regard no one from a human point of view…If anyone is *in Christ*, there is a *new creation….*"[3]

In **John 14:6-14** when Jesus "knew that his hour had come to depart from this world and go to the Father," he spoke about the mystery of believing in him:

> If you know me, you will *know my Father* also… I am in the Father and the Father is in me…. the one who believes in me will also do the works that I do and, in fact, will do *greater works than these…* I will ask the Father, and he will *give you another Advocate*, to be with you forever…. On that day you will know that I am in my Father, and *you in me, and I in you.*

Peter urged Baptism, not just so that our "sins may be forgiven." But also so that we may "receive the gift of the Holy Spirit." We die and rise in Christ to live a new life; one *visibly divine*. If the Spirit empowers us to know and act as only God can, this bears witness to the living presence of Jesus in us, who rose out of the waters of Baptism as his body risen from the grave. True *witnesses* live on the level of God.[4]

[1]For facts on St. James, see July 25 (next booklet).
[2]*Acts* 22:16; *1Peter* 3:18; *Romans* 6:3-7.
[3]*2Corinthians* 5:16-17.
[4]*Acts* 2:38.

Decision: Live a new life by the power of the Spirit. Go beyond being human.

SAME DAY MAY 3, 2011

The *Responsorial* (*Psalm* 93)—*"The Lord is king; he is robed in majesty"*— means Jesus is as different from earthly kings as God is different from his creatures. The Psalm continues: "He has established the world.... From everlasting you are.... Holiness belongs to your house...." And we are called to be as different from ordinary human beings as God is. How is that for a shocker?

Acts 4:32-37 shows us what it means to "bear witness to the resurrection of the Lord." It means to make it evident that Jesus is risen and living in us. We do that by living in a way that is both unintelligible and impossible without grace. And by "grace" we mean "the favor of sharing in the divine life of God." If we are not obviously divine, we are not the kind of humans God made and called us to be by Baptism.

The early "community of believers" was "of one heart and mind." That is the first sign of divine life. Jesus prayed at the Last Supper: "that they may all be one." Not just as a human community. He prayed that we might be one *as the Three Persons of the Holy Trinity are one*: "As you, Father, are in me and I am in you, may they also be in us." What does this say about us?[1]

On the visible, human level it should be evident that no human concerns have enough importance to divide us. Are we who are united by sharing in the divine life of God going to let ourselves be disunited by something that is of value only on the level of human life?

Jesus already laid down this principle in the "Sermon on the Mount":

> If anyone strikes you on the right cheek, turn the other also; and if anyone wants to sue you and take your coat, give your cloak as well; and if anyone forces you to go one mile, go also the second mile.

The general principle here is that for those who are the body of Christ on earth and children of God the Father, nothing on this earth should take precedence over good relationship with another human being. Not our wounded pride when we are insulted or feel rejection like a slap in the face. Not attachment to our possessions or the arrogance of someone cheating us out of them. Not the pressure people put on us by imposing on our time or making our work longer or harder. Our response to all that is to risk more rejection by sticking our neck out again; to give others more than they are trying to cheat us out of; to spend more time on people than they are already costing us.[2]

Is that human? No, that is to be divine. In the "community of believers... no one claimed anything as a personal possession, but they had everything in common.... There was no needy person among them." That is Christian witness.

In **John 3:7-15** Jesus asked Nicodemus, "You do not understand this?" Is he asking us that? Three words: "You are divine." Do you understand them? If not, why not? If you would, decide how you could. *"The Lord is king; he is robed in majesty."* Jesus will help you.

[1] *John* 17:16-23.
[2] *Matthew* 5:38-42.

Decision: Come to grips with being divine. What does it mean to be it? To live it?

MAY 4, 2011

In **Acts 5:17-26** God delivered the Apostles from prison the way Jesus was delivered from the tomb. The temple police reported, "We found the prison securely locked and the guards standing at the doors, but when we opened them, we found no one inside." When Jesus rose, those who went to the tomb found it likewise empty. And no explanation.

By Baptism we were freed from the prison of this world's limits and the tomb of its death. We went down into the water of Baptism as into the grave. When we rose out of that water, those who looked for the "old self" we used to be simply did not find us. Our "old self" was "crucified with Jesus so that the body of sin might be destroyed, and we might no longer be enslaved to sin." We "were taught to put away our former way of life," our "old self with its practices," to be "renewed in the spirit of our minds" and to "clothe ourselves with the new self which is being renewed in knowledge according to the image of its creator" and "created according to the likeness of God in true righteousness and holiness."

We need to be conscious of this when we present ourselves to be placed on the altar under the symbols of bread and wine. We are accepting to step out of the prison of our culture's darkness. To be free of its myopic attitudes and intramundane values. To embrace the "new self" that was given to us at Baptism and which is growing—gradually—"until all of us come to... the knowledge of the Son of God..." and the Father brings the "image of his Son to perfection within us." The *Presentation of Gifts* is a commitment to *ongoing conversion*.[1]

John 3:16-21 warns us that something in us may "prefer darkness to light." Not just because our "works are evil" and we don't want that fact exposed, even to ourselves. But also because prison protects us from challenge. To be locked into the laws and practices of "religion" with such a walled-in vision that nothing gets past them is to escape the unknown of conscious interaction and personal relationship with God. We focus so narrowly on *what* we do that no *who* even enters the equation. John says God sent his Son so that "the world might be saved through *him*" and "whoever believes in *him* will not be condemned." Unless our faith lets us know Jesus as a person, and our hope is to grow in intimacy with him until we love him passionately, we are "condemned" to the half-life of the Pharisees. This is the way, not of life but of the living dead. We may be alive by grace, but barely.

The "way of life" is the way of those hungry to know and do more; to chart their course by the "single star" of Jesus; to sail by the "wild winds" of the Spirit, "withersoever they blow." It is the freedom of "nothing left to lose," because all has been given for All. The *Responsorial* (*Psalm 34*) assures those who leave their measurable prison: *"The Lord hears the cry of the poor."*

[1] *Romans 6:6; Ephesians 4:13, 22-24; Colossians 3:9-10; Preface I for Lent.*

Decision: Give up security. Trust God calling you into the unknown.

MAY 5, 2011

Acts 5:27-33 presents us with a puzzle. The Apostles' strength came from their certitude they were speaking God's truth and doing God's will: "We must obey God rather than any human authority." Where did this certitude come from? Obviously, from the Holy Spirit. But Peter said God gave the Spirit "to those who obey him." So were the Apostles empowered to obey God rather than humans because they had the Holy Spirit, or did God give them the Spirit because they obeyed him?

This isn't just a word game. There is a mutual dependency between faith and action. Faith empowers us to act, but it is action that confirms us in faith. The Apostles knew their certitude was from the Holy Spirit when they took the action of risking prison and death by disobeying the human authorities.

How does this work?

By definition, faith is certitude about something beyond the reach of human reason, something that "transcends" the range of any creature's activity. John 3:31-36 insists on the contrast:

> The one who is of the earth belongs to the earth and speaks about earthly things. The one who comes from heaven is above all. He testifies to what he has seen and heard.

So how do we know that "the one who comes from heaven" is speaking to us and through us? That we are in a real, and not just an imagined relationship with the transcendent God?

First we consciously establish ourselves in a relationship with some visible, created person or reality. We can know this relationship is real, because the reality of relationship is *interaction* and we can experience ourselves interacting with visible people and things on this earth. But we make sure that what we are doing is such that there is simply no human reason for doing it, no value on earth that would motivate us to do it. Then we know we must be doing it for some value not of this earth, some "transcendent" value. That can only be God. God alone is "beyond" everything created. "The one who comes from heaven is above all." He alone.

So if we want to know we are in a real relationship with God—acting toward him with real faith, real hope, real love—the way to do it is to take a stance toward some created person or value that requires "as the condition for its possibility" the reality of the stance we want to take toward God. "We don't know we truly believe in the two birds in the bush until we let go of the one bird in the hand."

We experience the reality of our faith in the *act* of making *choices* that we would not (or could not) make without it.

That is why the *Presentation of Gifts* is such an important moment in the Mass. It is the moment that invites us to declare explicitly to God that we *choose* to participate in this celebration and in the mystery it expresses: the mystery of our baptismal incorporation into Christ, into his body, into his Church, into the mission he wants to continue in and through us as members of his risen body, anointed *prophets*, *priests*, and *stewards of his kingship*.

Decision: Empty yourself to know you are filled with the Spirit. The *Responsorial* (*Psalm* 34) promises, "*The Lord hears the cry of the poor.*"

MAY 6, 2011

The *Responsorial* (*Psalm* 27) tells us what each one is expressing during the *Presentation of Gifts: "One thing I seek: to dwell in the house of the Lord."*

Acts 5:34-42 gives us what is known as "the principle of Gamaliel":

> If this undertaking is of human origin, it will fail; but if it is of God, you will not be able to overthrow them—in that case you may even be found fighting against God!

This says that what God inspires people to do will not fail because of external opposition or lack of human resources. God's word achieves its end:

> For as the rain and the snow come down from heaven, and do not return there until they have watered the earth... giving seed to the sower and bread to the eater, so shall my word be that goes out from my mouth; it shall not return to me empty, but it shall accomplish that which I purpose, and succeed in the thing for which I sent it.

Jesus pointed out in the "Parable of the Sower" that God's word does not always bear fruit. But it only fails because of an internal failure of faith, hope, or love in those who deliver or receive the message.[1]

We express our faith in this principle every time we bring up the insignificant elements of bread and wine during the *Presentation of Gifts*, counting on them to become the mystery, the sacrifice that redeems the world. From a human point of view, isn't it ridiculous to think that a few pieces of bread and a cup of wine can achieve what all the money, talent, weapons, and technological wizardry of the world cannot achieve? But we believe it. Because this bread "will become for us the Bread of Life."

> For whatever is born of God conquers the world. And this is the victory that conquers the world, our faith.[2]

The Apostles, sentenced to be flogged,

> left the presence of the Sanhedrin rejoicing that they had been found worthy to suffer for the sake of the Name. And day after day, both in the temple and at home, they never stopped teaching and proclaiming the good news of Jesus the Messiah.

If faith is alive, we will conquer. If we are conquering, our faith must be alive.

In **John 6:1-15** the "multiplication of the loaves" depended on Jesus having some loaves to multiply. He didn't just produce them out of thin air.

He could have. But God has chosen and is still choosing to save the world with the help of the humans being saved. This saves our dignity as free persons and God's reputation as Creator. No matter how bad we are, our human nature is basically good and capable of cooperating freely with God.

Without the *Presentation of Gifts* there would not be any *Eucharistic Prayer*. If we don't present the bread—and ourselves as represented by it—the Bread of Life will not become present.

When the people "saw the sign Jesus had done," they said, "This is truly the Prophet who is to come into the world." Our task as "prophets in the Prophet" is to live in a way that shows Jesus is still in the world. We are empowered to do this by the "gift of the Spirit."

[1] *Isaiah* 55:9-11; *Matthew* 13:3-33.
[2] *1John* 5:4.

Decision: Live the impossible dream. Show that with God all things are possible.

MAY 7, 2011

Acts 6:1-7 shows us that, although all in the Church are equally Christ and equal members of his body, there are many different roles and functions in the Church, some of them incompatible with others. One role was that of the "Twelve," who were those apostles who had been chosen as special witnesses out of the disciples who had been with Jesus "beginning from the baptism of John until the day when he was taken up from us." They had the function of "overseers," but they could not be everywhere and oversee everything.[1]

So when argument broke out over the distribution of food they "called together the whole community of the disciples" and asked them to "select from among yourselves seven men... whom we may appoint to this task [of serving at tables], while we, for our part, will devote ourselves to prayer and to serving the word." Both functions are "service," *diakonia*. One is food service, the other "word service," but both services are equal, as are the persons chosen for each. They are like the hosts brought up in the *Presentation of Gifts:* are all distinct, but they are all one bread. All look alike, are treated alike, and all become equally the "Bread of life." St. Paul is clear about that:

I say to *everyone* among you not to think of yourself more highly than you ought to think.... For as in one body we have many members, and not all the members have the same function, so we, who are many, are one body in Christ, and individually we are members one of another.

We respect each one's role—in the Church and in civil society—without seeing anyone as "higher" or "lower" than anyone else: "Pay to all what is due them—taxes... revenue... respect... honor...." But what should dominate and characterize every relationship is love.

Owe no one anything, except to love one another; for the one who loves another has fulfilled the law.[2]

When persecution in Jerusalem caused the Greek-speaking Christians to flee to Samaria while the Twelve remained behind, those chosen for ministry at table took on the ministry of the word. Philip, especially, the first named, is described as preaching, baptizing, and "proclaiming the good news to all the towns."[3] As we saw in yesterday's Gospel (*John* 6:9), when there is need, the gifts are present in the community; we just have to use them.

In **John 6:16-21**, as soon as the disciples "wanted to take Jesus into the boat" they found they had already arrived where they wanted to go. We may wonder sometimes if we really are the kind of Christians we need to be—or if the Mass has any "meaning" for us. We need to be clear about the significance of *desire.* If we *want* to take Jesus into our hearts, *want* to "get something" out of the Mass, *want* it to have meaning for us, we are already "there." This is the value of "affective prayer" in the *Presentation of Gifts:* just *willing* and *offering* to be what Baptism made us, the body of Christ.

[1] *Acts* 1:20-22.
[2] *Romans* 12:1-10; 13:7-8. This is also the clear message of *1Corinthians*, chapters 12-13.
[3] *Acts* 8:4-40.

Decision: Be what you are and desire to become all God wants you to be.

FOR REFLECTION AND DISCUSSION: EASTER WEEK TWO

Experiencing and Expressing the Risen Life: We must "no longer look for Jesus among the dead"—including the deadening routine of just "saying prayers" or participating in Mass without attention—for "he has become the Lord of *life*."

Invitation:

Experience Christ's life within you by living as you couldn't without it.

Ask yourself in prayer and others in discussion: How could the statements below make Mass mean more if we stay aware of them during Mass?

Acts 4:23-31: We acknowledge in the *Presentation of Gifts* the most basic truth perceived by human intelligence: that nothing exists except by God's ongoing creative will: "Lord, God of all creation, through your goodness we have...."

John 3:1-8: By "presenting our bodies" under the form of bread to be offered as at Baptism, we reaffirm our faith that human life is meant to become divine life.

Acts 4:32-37: We "bear witness to the resurrection of the Lord" by living in a way that is both unintelligible and impossible unless Jesus is risen and living in us.

If we are not obviously divine, we are not the kind of humans Baptism made us.

The first sign of divine life is for the "community of believers" to be "of one heart and mind," showing that no human concerns have enough importance to divide us.

Acts 5:17-26: To *present* ourselves with the gifts is to pledge *ongoing conversion—* until the Father brings the "image of his Son to perfection within us."

Acts 5:27-33: Faith empowers us to act, but we experience faith as real in the *act* of making *choices* we would not (or could not) make without it.

The *Presentation of Gifts* is an important moment in the Mass because it invites us to declare explicitly to God, ourselves, and others that we *choose* to participate.

Acts 5:34-42: What God inspires will not fail because of external opposition or lack of human resources; only because of an internal failure of faith, hope, or love.

John 6:1-15: If we don't present the bread, Christ will not become present on the altar. If we don't present ourselves, Christ will not be present in the world.

Acts 6:1-7: We respect each one's role in the Church and in society without seeing anyone as "higher" than anyone else. All were just bread. Now all are Christ.

John 6:16-21: The value of "affective prayer" in the *Presentation of Gifts* is in the significance of *desire*. If we *want* the Mass to have meaning for us, then it does.

Decisions:

Take God's words seriously. Make some choices consciously based on them.
Recognize God as Creator by intelligence and as Father by faith.
Come to grips with being divine. What does it mean to be it? To live it?
Live the impossible dream. Show that with God all things are possible.
Be what you are and desire to become all God wants you to be.

May 8, 2011

Finding Joy in Christ

INVENTORY

What gives me the most joy in life? What do I do now to find joy? Have I ever decided on a formula for living a joyful life? Do I think religion is one?

INPUT

The *Entrance Antiphon* assumes the whole world should find joy in God: *"Let all the earth cry out to God with joy.... Proclaim his glorious praise."* And in the *Opening Prayer* we ask God to give us the kind of live, conscious hope in our own resurrection from the dead that, whether we are young or old, gives us the joy of eternal youth: *"May we look forward with hope to our resurrection, for you have made us your sons and daughters, and restored the joy of our youth."* We have everlasting life because we have "become Christ" (St. Augustine). We are children of God: because "in Christ," we are the "only-begotten Son of the Father." Because we are members of his risen body, we share in his own divine life, life eternal.

The *Responsorial* (*Psalm* 16) gives the theme of the readings: If we live as Christ now, we will have now the joy of his life: *"Lord, you will show us the path of life."*

JESUS GIVES LIFE:

Acts 2:14-33 tells us that Jesus has "made known to us the path of life." He did this, not only by his teachings, but above all by rising from the dead to show that he can give what he promises. Jesus is the Life: he "fills us with joy in his presence." And because he is the Life, we can be sure that his *Truth* is the *Way* that leads to Life (see *John* 14:6; *Psalm* 86:11; *Matthew* 22:16).

It is not only the testimony of Christ's resurrection that convinces us he is the Way, the Truth, and the Life. It is also, and most immediately, the testimony of the Holy Spirit poured out in our hearts. The evidence to which Peter appeals in his first public proclamation of the Good News is the double sign of Christ's *resurrection* and the *manifestation of the Spirit* in those who witnessed to him: *"God raised this Jesus*; of this we are all witnesses. Exalted at God's right hand, he received the *promise of the Holy Spirit* from the Father *and poured him forth, as you see and hear."*

For us to bear witness to Christ as *prophets*, our lives have to be visible proof of the presence of Christ's Holy Spirit in us. To do this we must show in our body language, words, and actions the "fruit of the Spirit": "love, joy, peace, patience, kindness, generosity, faithfulness, gentleness, and self-control" (*Galatians* 5:22). For now let us focus on *joy*.

REALIZING...

1Peter 1:17-21 tells us how to do this.

29

It is not by "projecting an image" of joy; it is by *realizing*, remaining *conscious* that we have been "ransomed from the futile ways inherited from our ancestors, not with... silver or gold, but with the precious blood of Christ."

We read last Sunday, "In this you rejoice, even if now for a little while you have had to suffer various trials, so that *the genuineness of your faith...* tested by fire, may... result in praise and glory and honor when Jesus Christ is revealed."

What makes our witness credible makes our joy a reality: "Although you have not seen him, you love him; and even though you do not see him now, you believe in him and rejoice with an indescribable and glorious joy, for you are *receiving the outcome of your faith*, the salvation of your souls" (*1Peter* 1:6-9). We have joy, even when things are very difficult or painful for us, because we "believe in God who raised Jesus from the dead and gave him glory, so that our faith and hope are in God"—not in anything this world gives or promises.

THEY RECOGNIZED HIM:

Luke 24:13-35 shows us how we come to this faith and hope. It is first through *encounter with Jesus*: "Jesus drew near and walked with them."

Secondly, it is through *intellectual understanding*: "He interpreted to them what referred to him in all the Scriptures." But intellectual knowledge is not enough; we have to experience God himself speaking to us through the Scriptures. It is a mystery and mystical experience of *encounter*: "Were not our hearts burning within us *while he spoke to us* on the way and opened the Scriptures to us?"

Finally, we have to *celebrate* what we have experienced. We have to re-express it in our own words, and in more than words. Celebration involves the whole person: body, emotions, mind, and will, and action. The deepest (and most available!) celebration is *Eucharist*. The disciples did not really recognize Jesus until he *"took bread, said the blessing, broke it, and gave it to them"*—the Gospel formula for Eucharist. "With that their eyes were opened and they recognized him."

We too know Jesus "in the breaking of the bread." It is in the Mass that we express and experience the mystery of our faith most clearly, most deeply, in its fullness. For this, however, we have to give "full, conscious, active" *participation*. We have to listen to the words, be aware of what they mean, try to mean them more every time we say them, make the Mass an authentic expression of our own faith, hope, and love. Then in the Mass the *"Lord will show us the path of life."*

INSIGHT
What in my religion gives me joy? What else would if I focused on it with faith?

INITIATIVE
Decide to identify and absorb everything in my religion that is a source of joy.

MAY 9, 2011

The *Responsorial* (*Psalm* 119) confronts us with an either-or choice: *"Blessed are they who follow the law of the Lord."* Either we have decided to do that or we haven't. If we have, we need to begin with what God says we should live for.

In **John 6:22-29** Jesus is blunt about what should be the goal of our life: "Do not work for the food that perishes, but for the food that endures for eternal life." He is equally blunt about where we find that food. It is "…what the Son of Man will give you."

There it is: an either-or choice. Take it or leave it.

It is quite possible many of us have never confronted that choice. Not seriously. Not explicitly, as a crucial decision we have to make. ("Crucial" comes from *crux*, meaning "cross." A "crucial" decision is one we face at the crossroads of life. A direction-setter).

Why are so few teenagers interested in reflections like these? It is because many are not conscious of setting a direction for life. They have short-term goals: text a friend, pass a test, take a trip, work on their appearance, make a team, win a game. At most they may be thinking of getting into a particular college or preparing for some career. Some may identify fulfillment in life with a career or a happy marriage. Pitiful, but true. Few even suspect there is a larger picture. They are not looking for anything except what "perishes."

And let's be honest: the last place they think they will find real joy and fulfillment in life is through relationship with Jesus Christ.

Let's be even more honest. In this, aren't most adults little better than teenagers?

Acts 6:8-15 invites us to look at self-identity. People are willing to murder Stephen just because he is calling into question their national and religious identity as Jews. They see him changing who they are. He is threatening their religion, nationality, and culture all combined. They will kill him for it.

Most of us grew up with three identities we took for granted: *family, nationality,* and *religion*. Would you kill to keep living as an American? As a Christian? As a (insert your family name)? Would you die rather than give up any one of them? Have you ever really thought about what each one means in your life? You received all three without choosing. Have you ever personally, consciously, deeply chosen one or all of them?

In every Mass the *Presentation of Gifts* invites you to choose your religion. Deeply and personally. Do you do it? Do you place yourself on the altar each time, with the host that represents you, to offer yourself to God as you did at Baptism? Do you focus all your life's hopes on what "the Son of Man will give you?" Does desire for this rule every choice of your life?

Or would you have to say, to be truly honest, that in what is most important in life you are not really looking further ahead than a teenager?

If you participate in Mass "fully, actively, and consciously," the *Presentation of Gifts* will give and sustain focus in your life.

Decision: Don't fly blind. Focus on the goal and keep your eyes on it.

May 10, 2011

The *Responsorial* (*Psalm* 31) is the profession of faith and trust Jesus made before he died; except he called God "Father" instead of "Lord": *"Into your hands, O Lord, I commend my spirit."* The meaning of the whole Psalm is summed up in the next-to-last verse: "Be strong, and let your heart take courage, all you who wait for the Lord."

In **Acts 7:51 to 8:1** Stephen died with the same words on his lips except he addressed them to Jesus: "Lord Jesus, receive my spirit." These are the words of ultimate faith, hope, and love. To say them with our last breath is to die a Christian death. To say them with every breath we take is to live a Christian life. This is the meaning of the traditional greeting and prayer at Mass: "The Lord be with you," with its echo: "And with your spirit." What it says is, "Be strong, and let your heart take courage, all you who wait for the Lord. He is here."

The "people, elders, and scribes"[1] killed Stephen because he said, "you always oppose the Holy Spirit." Their whole religion focused on keeping the law, but Stephen said "you did not observe it" because they did not let the Holy Spirit show them what it meant. Law observance without intimate knowledge of the mind and heart of God is deadly. These are the ones who persecute the prophets in every age.

This is a reason why at Mass, after hearing God's words in the readings, we symbolically place ourselves on the altar in the *Presentation of Gifts* to be *transformed*. As the bread that represents us is changed into the Bread of life, God promises we will be changed:

A new heart I will give you, and a new spirit I will put within you.... I will put my spirit within you, and make you follow my statutes and be careful to observe my ordinances.. Then [you] shall be my people, and I will be [your] God.[2]

The words the presider speaks in the name of all during the *Presentation of Gifts* echo the words of Jesus in **John 6:30-35**: "I am the Bread of Life."

Blessed are you, Lord... through your goodness we have this bread to offer... It will become for us the Bread of Life.

We don't just present ourselves in commitment to give human obedience to the words of Jesus as understood by our human minds. St. Paul tells us, "Present your bodies as a living sacrifice" to be

transformed by the renewing of your minds, so that you may discern what is the will of God—what is good and acceptable and perfect.

We are committing ourselves to live out our baptismal consecration as *prophets*. We seek *enlightenment* through God's word as *disciples*, but we know we will not truly understand how to live as *witnesses* to Jesus Christ until we have been "clothed with power from on high" by the "gift of the Spirit." We receive it through *surrender*: *"Into your hands, O Lord, I commend my spirit."*[3]

---

[1] Modern equivalents are "laity, clergy, and Canon lawyers." The correct word for ordained priests is "presbyters" or "elders." The scribes were the teachers or "doctors" of the law. The Gospels link the "scribes and Pharisees" together as allies twenty times.
[2] *Ezekiel* 11:19; 36:26.
[3] *Romans* 12:1-2; *Luke* 24:48-49; *Acts* 1:8; 2:38; 10:45; *1Corinthians* 2:6-16.

Decision: Obey laws, not according to their letter but by the Spirit.

MAY 11, 2011

The *Responsorial* (*Psalm* 66) extends Easter joy to every creature: "*Let all the earth cry out to God with joy.*" The key to this joy is *seeing* and *believing*. The Psalm continues: "Come and *see* the works of God…. Therefore let us *rejoice* in him."

Acts 8:1-8 shows us Philip, who was chosen for the administrative task of distributing food, "proclaiming the good news about the kingdom of God and the name of Jesus Christ" and baptizing. "Philip went down to… Samaria and proclaimed the Christ to them."[1]

Philip and the others with him were doing all of this as what we call "laypersons."[2] Church rules and customs change with the times, but it is important to remember that according to our *theology,* all of the baptized are consecrated and empowered as *prophets* to bear witness to Jesus Christ in word and action. Anyone can validly baptize, although the Church has prudently ruled that for Catholics this should normally take place and be registered only in a parish and under the jurisdiction of a pastor. Likewise, during Mass the specific preaching of "homilies" is restricted by current rules to the clergy. We should not let this make us forget, however, that by Baptism we are *all* charged to preach the Gospel and teach each other the word of God in every possible way. We are *prophets*:

> Let the word of Christ dwell in you richly; teach and admonish one another in all wisdom; and with gratitude in your hearts sing psalms, hymns, and spiritual songs to God.[3]

It would be a natural mistake to see in the *Presentation of Gifts* only the "administrative" action of preparing the altar and bringing up the gifts. All present need to remind themselves to enter into this moment with minds and hearts alert to the spiritual meaning embodied in the actions. We present *ourselves* under the symbols of bread and wine to be offered with Christ and in Christ during the *Eucharistic Prayer*. This is a peak moment of Mass: "*Let all the earth cry out to God with joy.*"

In **John 6:35-40** Jesus promises: "I am the bread of life. Whoever comes to me will never hunger, and whoever believes in me will never thirst." This obviously invites us to deep, personal, direct interaction with Jesus in everything we do. But it also makes us conscious that many people will "come to Jesus," especially in the beginning of their faith journey, only by seeing him in others who are his body and real presence on earth. To "see" him they must have faith. But they will find faith by seeing faith *embodied* in the lifestyle of those who already have it. This defines our role as *prophets*: to live in such a way that our life can only be explained by Christ living within us. It is to this that we pledge ourselves at the *Presentation of Gifts*.

[1]Verse 12. See *Acts* 6:1-6; 8:26-40; 21:8.
[2]The identification of "deacons" with the "seven" chosen in *Acts* 6:1-6 is not Scriptural.
[3]*Colossians* 3:16. See also *2Timothy* 2:2; *1John* 2:27; *Hebrews* 8:10-11. See the *Catechism of the Catholic Church,* nos. 436, 1241, 1268.

Decision: Let people see Jesus as the only explanation of what they see in you.

MAY 12, 2011

The *Responsorial* (*Psalm* 66) repeats yesterday's theme:— "*Let all the earth cry out to God with joy.*"

Acts 8:26-40 shows one of the shortest versions of the RCIA on record. Philip explained the Scriptures to the court official. He believed, asked for baptism, received it and "continued on his way rejoicing"—back to Ethiopia. There wasn't even any follow-up. "The Spirit of the Lord snatched Philip away and the eunuch saw him no more."

Today we require a lot more instruction before Baptism. For adults, at least. For infants the rule is that we only baptize children when there is reasonable certitude they will be instructed and formed in the faith by their parents.

But what follow-up is there for adults once they are baptized and confirmed? Is Sunday Mass enough? Let's not discount the continuing formation we receive through the practices of the liturgical seasons: Advent, Christmas, Easter, Pentecost, "Ordinary Time," and the various feast days that emphasize some major event or doctrine. Still, is it enough?

It may not be. Some kind of more personal community interaction in the family or in small groups may be necessary. But if we learn to participate fully in the Mass, understanding what is really going on and consciously involving ourselves in the action, we will experience the Eucharist more and more as what it is: the "source and summit of the Christian life."

In these *Reflections* we focus during Advent-Christmas on the *Introductory Rites* and *evangelization*: on the *new identity* we have in Christ. During Lent, on the *Liturgy of the Word* and *discipleship*: the experience of *enlightenment*. During Easter on the *Presentation of Gifts* and prophetic *witness*: the call to lead a *lifestyle* empowered by the Gift of the Spirit. During Ordinary Time (Weeks 11-22), on the *Eucharistic Prayer* and the call to *minister* as *priests* by Baptism. During Weeks 23-34, on the *Rite of Communion* and on *leadership* in establishing the reign of God as *stewards* of Christ's kingship. Over the course of a year these reflections will imbue us with the spirit of the Mass.

In **John 6:44-51** Jesus says, "No one can come to me unless drawn by the Father." At Mass be conscious that the Father himself has drawn you there. Praise and thank him for this during the *Introductory Rites*.

"They shall all be taught by God." God is fulfilling this promise during the *Liturgy of the Word*. Listen to learn.

"Not that anyone has seen the Father...." During the *Presentation of Gifts* present yourself for progressive conversion to a lifestyle that makes God more and more visible in you as *prophet*.

"I am the bread of life." During the *Eucharistic Prayer* offer your "flesh for the life of the world" as *priest*.

"Whoever eats this bread will live forever." Receive *Communion* as a foretaste of the Kingdom. Pledge yourself as a *steward of Christ's kingship* to keep working for his reign.

Decision: Make the Mass the "source and summit" of your life. Learn how.

MAY 13, 2011

The *Response* (*Mark* 16:15, used with *Psalm* 117) is our life: *"Go out to all the world and tell the Good News."*

Acts 9:1-20 is the source of everything Paul preached: "I am *Jesus, whom you are persecuting."* From the first, Paul knew Jesus as identified with us.

Paul could have answered, "I am not persecuting you. I am persecuting your followers." But he didn't, because he understood immediately, and more deeply than he had ever understood anything in his life, what Jesus was saying. Those who receive the life of God in Baptism *"become Christ."* This is the "mystery hidden throughout the ages and generations but now revealed." The mystery Paul was sent to preach is simply *"Christ in you, the hope of glory."* That is how Paul identified himself: "It is no longer I who live, but it is Christ who lives in me." We must see and identify ourselves in the same way: as people who have *"become Christ."*[1]

When Ananias laid hands on Paul, "something like scales fell from his eyes." This is what happens to us when we finally recognize the true mystery of Baptism and realize that we have "become Christ." We recognize what Paul meant when he said "You have *come to fullness* in him." And "God has *made you alive* together with him." "Continue to *live your lives in him*" as his living, risen body on earth.[2]

Then we understand our life as mission: *"Go out to all the world and tell the Good News."* The Church "exists to evangelize." The Church is us.[3]

What does it take to make the scales fall from our eyes? The truth is, most of us do not think of ourselves as "being Christ." As Christians, yes. Or "Catholics" (or Methodists, Baptists, Presbyterians, etc.). And if asked what that meant, we would probably list the doctrines, rules, and practices that belong to our "religion." How many would say, "It means I try to be conscious of Christ acting *with* me, *in* me, and *through* me all day long"? How many could honestly say, "It means that in everything I do I try consciously to act "through him, with him, and in him" as his risen body on earth"? There are scales on our eyes. Scales of superficial religious instruction. Scales of cultural conditioning. Scales of shortsighted preoccupation with "the cares of the world, the lure of wealth, and desire for other things" that blind us to mystery. Do we even know we are blind?[4]

The blind in **John 6:52-59** ask: "How can this man give us his flesh to eat?" The *Presentation of Gifts* should open our eyes to ask: "If the bread we present becomes the Body of Christ, can't *we* in a real way 'become Christ' by Baptism?" We grow to appreciate *how* we who "eat his flesh 'abide in him and he in us'" by staying *conscious* of Jesus acting *with* us, *in* us, and *through* us in everything we do. We grow into it.

---

[1] See the *Catechism of the Catholic Church* 795, 460; *Colossians* 1:25-28; *Galatians* 2:19-20.
[2] See *Colossians* 2:6-13.
[3] Paul VI, *Evangelization in the Modern World*, no. 14.
[4] *Mark* 4:19. Read the whole parable.

Decision: Identify yourself. Be comfortable saying, "I have become Christ."

MAY 14, 2011

Feast of Saint Matthias, Apostle

The *Responsorial* (*Psalm* 113) applies to Matthias: *"The Lord will give him a seat with the leaders of his people."*

The selection of Matthias to replace Judas in **Acts 1:15-26** shows that bishops are not "successors" to the Twelve Apostles. Although "the phrase is too well attested to be rejected now," if it is "used without care for the finer distinctions it may distort the truth."

> The apostles could never have a successor in that function of witness which was at the heart of their calling (*Acts* 2:32; 3:15; 4:20-33; 8:25; 10:39-42; 13:31). They are those who bear witness to the fact that the risen Lord is the Jesus in whose company they had lived (*Acts* 1:21-22). That is why to have been with Jesus during his life and after his death [as Matthias was] remained a qualification essential in anyone who was to be included in the group of the [twelve] apostles and to take part in the first mission, that of bearing witness (*Acts* 1:1-3; 10:41)…. This is why the twelve are forever, once and for all… the Church's foundation. No one could follow them in this function of witness.

The bishops are not "successors" but "*vicars*" of the Twelve; that is, someone who "acts in place of" another. As vicars, what the bishops "succeed" to is the "*function* of shepherding and teaching in order to guard the churches founded on the power of [the apostles'] witness." And this function is a daunting one! Bishops need all the help and encouragement we can give them.[1]

Over the centuries the popes have appropriated to themselves some of the powers that properly belong to the heads of the local churches; for example, the right to decide whom to ordain as priests and how to train them. The bishops must provide "enough priests capable of properly caring for the people of God," but from a pool severely restricted by papal preferences. Other Vatican preferences limit the bishops' authority as "the governors… and guardians of the entire liturgical life in the church committed to them." More radically, the popes have made all bishops papal appointees, having taken away the local churches' power to select their own bishops that "for the first thousand years of Church history" was "clearly recognized…. It was only in 1884 that the papacy claimed the right to name bishops throughout the world."[2]

For perspective, we read **John 15:9-17:** Jesus says the Church should "keep his commandments" as he kept his Father's: not as "slaves" but as "friends" who "know what their master is about" and "live in his love." His commandment is, "Love one another as I have loved you." Bishops and pastors should govern as "friends," sharing their intentions, motives, and decisions transparently with the flock in "mutual trust."[3] Christ wants us to live in such a way that our "joy may be complete" and we will "bear fruit." These are the signs of a healthy Church. They are goals that as *prophets* we must work for.

[1] J.M.R. Tillard, O.P., *The Bishop of Rome*, pp. 93-96. For the impossible load placed on bishops, see *Vatican II.* "Decree on Bishops in the Church," ch. 2, nos. 12-18.
[2] *Loc. cit.* nos. 15, 22. T. Rausch, *Catholicism in the Third Millennium*, Liturgical Press, 2003, pp. 218-19.
[3] *Vatican II*, "Bishops," no. 16.

Decision: Be faithful to the word and Spirit of God. Judge everything by them.

S<small>AME</small> D<small>AY</small> M<small>AY</small> 14, 2011

The *Responsorial* (*Psalm* 116), asks: *"How shall I make a return to the Lord for all the good he has done for me?"* The answer is "Get up!"

Acts 9:31-42 shows us Peter healing a bedridden man and raising a woman who had died. His command to both was the same: *anastathi*, "Rise!" "Get up!"[1] The point is, they didn't know they were healed until they did. And if we want to experience Christ giving us new life, the way to do it is to "get up" and go: *do* something, live the life of grace, spread the Good News, *act*. No one ever rose from the dead by staying inert in a coffin. *"How shall I make a return to the Lord for all the good he has done for me?"* Yesterday's *Responsorial* gave the answer: *"Go out to all the world and tell the Good News."* Commit yourself to *mission*.

John 6:60-69 parallels the "confession of faith" that in *Matthew* 16:16 got Peter named pope. In *Matthew* Peter's reply of faith in Jesus precedes the announcement that Jesus is going to be a savior who wins by losing, triumphing through crucifixion. Peter finds this too shocking to accept, just as Christians today find the similar concept of nonviolence—accepting to be killed rather than to kill—too shocking to accept. Peter's confession of faith in Jesus as Messiah turns immediately into rejection of the kind of Messiah Jesus is going to be. "No! God forbid!"

In John what shocks people is Eucharist: "How can this man give us his flesh to eat?" Even "many of his disci-

ples said, 'This teaching is difficult; who can accept it?'" And "many turned back and no longer went about with him." But this time Peter came through. When Jesus "asked the Twelve, 'Do you also wish to go away?' Simon Peter answered, 'Lord, to whom can we go? You have the words of eternal life.'"

In *John* it is in the context of Eucharist that Jesus describes Peter's special role in the Church. After the Resurrection Jesus asks Peter three times if he loves him. This was probably to give him a chance, without making a point of it, to make up for his three denials. And each time, when Peter says he does, Jesus answers: "Feed my sheep."

He also predicts that Peter will embrace the fate he objected so much to Jesus embracing. The Bread of life is the fruit of death. Like Jesus, to "feed the flock" Peter will pay with his blood.

For those charged with pastoral ministry, this is the "first and greatest commandment." In order to "love the Lord your God with all your heart... and your neighbor as yourself," Jesus tells them, "Feed my sheep." Woe to those who deny the Eucharist to anyone without certain and serious cause.[2]

When Peter objected to the sacrificial core of the *Eucharistic Prayer*: "Lord! This must never happen to you!" Jesus flayed him: "Get behind me, Satan! You are a stumbling block to me!" What will he say to those who in the *Rite of Communion* refuse to "feed his sheep"?

[1]Several saints were named Anastasius or Anastasia, for "Risen" with Christ.
[2]*Matthew*: 24:40; *John* 21:1-19

Decision: Get up and give whatever it takes to "feed the sheep."

37

FOR REFLECTION AND DISCUSSION: EASTER WEEK THREE

The Third Week of Easter: The whole world should find joy in God. We have everlasting life and are children of God because we are "in Christ," the "only-begotten Son of the Father." We have "become Christ" (St. Augustine). The Spirit in our hearts bears witness to Christ's divine life in us, revealed in words and actions that show the "fruit of the Spirit," one of which is *joy.*

Invitation: By full, active, conscious participation, make the Mass a true *celebration*: using *memory* for *encounter* with Christ (*Introductory Rites*); *intellect* for deeper *understanding* (*Liturgy of the Word*); and *will* for joyful *recommitment (Presentation of Gifts).*

Ask yourself in prayer and others in discussion: How could the statements below make Mass mean more if we stay aware of them during Mass?

Acts 6:8-15: In every Mass the *Presentation of Gifts* invites us to choose our religious identity. **John 6:22-29:** The key is in what we decide to live for.

Acts 7:51 to 8:1: A religion of law observance alone is deadly. We must be "transformed by the renewing of our minds." We ask this in the *Presentation of Gifts* by uniting ourselves to the bread that will become the Bread of Life.

Acts 8:1-8: All Christians, even those in administrative functions, see themselves as evangelizers; just as in the "administrative" action of preparing the altar during the *Presentation of Gifts* we see the spiritual meaning embodied in the actions.

Acts 8:26-40: The Mass, as the "source and summit of the Christian life," is the best follow-up to Baptism if we pay attention to all it expresses: *New identity* as Christ (*Introductory Rites*); *Discipleship* (*Liturgy of the Word*); *Continual conversion* as *prophets* (*Presentation of Gifts*); surrender to *Ministry* as *priests* (*Eucharistic Prayer*); *Leadership* as *stewards* of the reign of God (*Rite of Communion*).

Acts 9:1-20: The core of everything St. Paul preached was our identification with Christ. The *Presentation of Gifts* should open our eyes to the mystery that we "become Christ" by Baptism as truly as the bread becomes his Body.

Acts 9:31-42: The way to experience Christ giving us new life is to get up and go: *do* something, live the life of grace, spread the Good News, *act.*

Decisions:

Decide to identify and absorb everything in your religion that is a source of joy.
Don't fly blind. Focus on the goal and keep your eyes on it.
Obey laws, not according to their letter but by the Spirit.
Let people see Jesus as the only explanation of what they see in you.
Make the Mass the "source and summit" of your life. Learn how.
Identify yourself. Be comfortable saying, "I have become Christ."
Get up and give whatever it takes to "feed the sheep."

MAY 15, 2011

Jesus Is The Shepherd Who Leads Us To Life

INVENTORY

Where is my religion taking me? Do I experience it as leading me somewhere besides heaven? Where am I this year as compared to last year? Did I get there by consciously, explicitly following Christ? In what ways?

INPUT

The *Entrance Antiphon* speaks of an active, dynamic God: "The earth is full of the goodness of the Lord" because "by the word of the Lord the heavens *were made*"—and are still being made, being sustained in existence by the presence and action of God in the universe.

In the *Opening Prayer*, when we ask God through "Christ our shepherd" to "*lead us* to join the saints in heaven," we are asking him to lead us in the way we live our lives *on earth*. All who are alive are *in statu viae*: "in the condition of being on the road." Both *Vatican II*, (*The Church*, chapter VII) and the *liturgy* (*Eucharistic Prayer* III) call us a "pilgrim Church." We believe Jesus is leading us somewhere. To be a Christian is to follow, to *move*. Jesus is shepherd who leads us.

SAVING SHEPHERD:

The *Responsorial* (*Psalm* 23) focuses on a God who doesn't just dish up the same old feedlot fare every day, but who constantly *leads* us into richer religious experiences, into a more fulfilling spirituality—the way a shepherd leads sheep to higher, more nourishing pastures. "*The Lord is my shepherd; there is nothing I shall want.*"

Acts 2:14, 36-41 identifies Jesus as the shepherd who leads us out of enslavement to a corrupt and corrupting society. He died and rose from the dead so that we might "*Repent* [accept a complete change of goal and focus in life]…, be *baptized*…, receive the gift of the *Holy Spirit*…," and "*save* ourselves from this corrupt generation."

HEALING SHEPHERD:

1Peter 2:20-25 tells us that because of his sufferings, Jesus is able to *heal* us: "By his wounds you have been healed" (and see *Matthew* 8:16-17). But to be healed we have to *follow* him as sheep follow a shepherd. If we stay close to him he can keep us safe: "For you had gone astray like sheep, but you have now returned to the shepherd and guardian of your souls." We are healed, not by a one-time jolt from on high, but by a continuous process of *following* Jesus. This involves: 1. *interacting* with him, giving him an active part as *Savior* in everything we do; 2. *learning* from him as *disciples*; 3. accepting *empowerment* from the Holy Spirit to give flesh to his words in action as *prophets*; 4. loving and *ministering* to each other as *priests in the Priest*; and 5. *working*

39

with him as *stewards of his kingship* to establish the reign of God on earth. If this puts us on a collision course with society, so be it: "For to this you have been called."

"LIFE TO THE FULL"

It is all a matter of what voice or voices we choose to listen to. **John 10:1-10** alerts us that there are all sorts of people offering us role-models and remedies to boost us toward fulfillment; all sorts of guides and gurus proposing themselves as shepherds. How can we know which ads, which programs, which guidelines to believe in; which voices to trust, which crowd to follow? (Or, if we think we are not "followers," which crowd to run with? It usually means the same thing in practice).

The Gospel directs us to look at what *gate* the would-be shepherds are coming through. Are they using our desire for *money* as an approach? Our fear of *failure*? Our ambition to *succeed*? Our need to *belong*? To what in us are they appealing when they hold out their promises? What door, what gate are they holding open for us and inviting us to walk through?

Jesus says, "*I am the gate* for the sheep. Whoever enters through me will be saved... and find pasture." Whatever is proposed to us as an object of choice or a course to follow, we should ask whether the basic motivation for it is grounded in values taught by Jesus. We should not expect that commercials and advertisements should explicitly base themselves on religious values. That could turn into distasteful fundamentalism or a sacrilegious prostitution of religion. But *we ourselves* should *question and look* to see what underlying assumptions support the motivation presented to us. What do the advertisers—and what do our family, friends, and business associates—assume we want out of life? What do they think will give us happiness? What do they think will lead us to it? What carrot are the would-be shepherds dangling before us? What stick are they using to compel us?

The bottom line is: "Where are they leading us? What, ultimately, is being promised?" Jesus makes his promise explicit and clear: "*I came that they might have life* and have it more abundantly"—or in the 1980 edition of the *New American Bible*, "have it to the full."

Anyone who looks for the fullness of life through association and interaction with Jesus Christ will inevitably be a *prophet*—and probably pay the prophet's price. But the price buys "life to the full," both here and hereafter. If "*the Lord is my shepherd, there is nothing I shall want.*"

INSIGHT

What is "wanting" to those who follow Jesus? What to those who do not?

INITIATIVE

Be conscious you are moving. Keep looking ahead to see where you are going, and back to see where you have been.

MAY 16, 2011

The *Responsorial* (*Psalm* 42) specifies the effect the *Liturgy of the Word* should have on us: *"Athirst is my soul for the living God."* Like the disciples on the road to Emmaus, as God speaks to us through the readings, we should find ourselves saying, "Were not our hearts burning within us... while he was opening the scriptures to us?"[1]

In **Acts 11:1-18** the same thing happened to the Gentiles to whom Peter was sent to explain the Good News of Jesus. "While Peter was still speaking, the Holy Spirit fell upon all who heard the word," and they began "speaking in tongues and extolling God." Faced with this, Peter set aside all the rules and policies: "'Can anyone withhold the water for baptizing these people who have received the Holy Spirit just as we have?' So he ordered them to be baptized in the name of Jesus Christ."[2]

This was a major conversion on Peter's part, and it led to a community decision that defined the Church as "catholic."[3] Peter—and after him the Church—realized that Christianity was not identified with keeping the Jewish rules and customs all the first Christians had grown up with, such as circumcision, dietary laws, prescribed sacrifices and devotional practices. It started when God told Peter in a vision to eat food the Jews were forbidden to eat. "What God has made clean, you must not call profane." Obedience to the Spirit takes precedence over obedience to the Law, even though both are from God.

When did we learn this? When did our obedience to the word of God become personal response to God's living voice? When did we, as *disciples*, develop into *prophets*? When did we learn, in keeping laws, to look first to their goal, and to respond, not to their letter, but to the mind and heart of God behind them? This was our passage into maturity.

We express this liturgically in the *Presentation of Gifts*, which follows the *Liturgy of the Word*. Having heard God's living voice in the readings, we present ourselves to be transformed—not just the way human choices based on human understanding can change us, but as the bread which represents us will be transformed from bread "earth has given" into the "Bread of life." We who have already "become Christ" by Baptism recommit to living by the Spirit as *prophets*, living on the level of God.

In **John 10:1-10** Jesus tells us, "Whoever does not enter the sheepfold by the gate... is a thief and a bandit." Later he clarifies, "I am the gate. Whoever enters through me will be safe." Safe from what?

From everything, really. But in the context, what keeps us safe from the deadly virus of *legalism* in the Church—the temptation to focus our religion on observing rules—is personal relationship with Christ. Only through direct, constant, personal interaction with the person of Jesus as *prophets* can we "recognize his voice."

[1] *Luke* 24:32.
[2] Read *Acts*, chapter 10.
[3] See *Acts* 15:1-33.

Decision: Focus on Jesus. Let everything follow from this. Use the "WIT" prayer all day long: "Lord, do this *with* me, do this *in* me, do this *through* me.

MAY 17, 2011

The *Responsorial verse* is from *Psalm* 117:1 and *Romans* 15:11: *"All you nations, praise the Lord."* The rest of the *Responsorial* is from *Psalm* 87, which in the present context proclaims the *Church* the true home of all believers. A motive to "Go out to all the world and tell the Good News."

The three steps of evangelization are (1) *pre-evangelization* through an event (or lifestyle) that raises questions.[1] In **Acts 11:19-26** the Christians who were "scattered" by persecution to "Phoenicia, Cyprus, and Antioch" were the event. When people asked them why they were running, their answer was (2) *evangelization*: to explain about Jesus. Result: "a great number believed and were converted." Then they could (3) celebrate together in *eucharist*.

The witness that won people to join the Christians was not just the event that raised questions. It was the evident faith the Christians had and the joy they took in it. Plus the joy the "Church in Jerusalem" showed by welcoming them into unity and sending Barnabas as an official representative to confirm their acceptance by the whole Church.

This acceptance is a pattern:

> When the apostles at Jerusalem heard that Samaria had accepted the word of God, they sent Peter and John to them. The two went down and prayed for them that they might receive the Holy Spirit (for as yet the Spirit had not come upon any of them; they had only been baptized in the name of the Lord Jesus). Then Peter and John laid their hands on them, and they received the Holy Spirit.[2]

The Sacrament of "Confirmation" is not primarily the act of those who receive it "confirming" their acceptance of the Church; it is the act of someone who can speak for the whole Church as bishops do, confirming the membership in the Church that anyone can give to another through Baptism. It is the whole Church approving and, like Barnabas in Antioch, "encouraging all to remain firm in their commitment to the Lord."

Confirmation should give us a sense of being accepted as authentic Christians by someone with authority to judge and accept us in the name of the Church. At the same time, it encourages us to take our place in the ranks of those who carry on the Church's *mission*. It approves us as working members of the Church and confirms our anointing to take part in the triple task of Jesus as *Prophet*, *Priest*, and *King*.

John 10:22-30: Jesus is asked, "If you are the Messiah, tell us plainly."

At every Mass the *Presentation of Gifts* invites us to "tell plainly" that we accept Jesus as Messiah. This involves embracing his *mission* as defined in the "messianic anointing" of Baptism: "As Christ was anointed Priest, Prophet, and King, so live always as members of his body."[3] We "go up" symbolically with the bread and wine to commit ourselves to prophetic *witness*, *ministry*, and *leadership* in establishing his Kingdom.

[1] See *Acts* 2:4-8; 3:1-12; Pope Paul VI, *Evangelization in the Modern World*, no. 21.
[2] *Acts* 8:14-17.
[3] See *Catechism of the Catholic Church*, 695, 1241.

Decision: Ask if you have reason to be glad you are Christian. If so, express it.

MAY 18, 2011

The *Responsorial* (*Psalm* 67) is still celebrating the Good News and its extension to the whole world: *"O God, let all the nations praise you."*

The Psalm specifies, "May your *way be known* upon earth, among all nations your *salvation*." This inspires evangelization: we want every nation to "be glad and exult," accepting Christ who "rules with justice" and "guides" to salvation. We dedicate our lives to this!

Acts 12:24 to 13:5 shows the Spirit telling the Church in Antioch to dedicate Barnabas and Saul (Paul):

> While they were worshiping the Lord and fasting, the Holy Spirit said, "Set apart for me Barnabas and Saul for the work to which I have called them." Then after fasting and praying they laid their hands on them and sent them off.

Notice that it was the *Church* that "sent them off." The community. Not God or the Spirit acting directly on Paul and Barnabas as individuals. Not just an authority or bishop. The Spirit spoke to and through the community.

This may not be so visible today. When do we find the community, or a parish council, or the presbyterate and lay leaders assembled with the bishop "worshiping the Lord and fasting" to seek God's guidance in pastoral ministry? (Think about that. It may be happening in your parish and diocese without being recognized as such).

There is, however, a visible sign of it at every Mass. When the bread and wine are brought forward in the *Presentation of Gifts*, they are brought up from the back of the church, passing through the whole congregation. This says two things: first, that the whole congregation is "coming forward" symbolically to place themselves on the altar under the signs of the bread and wine. But it also says that each individual, represented by each individual host, is being presented by the whole community. We don't go forward only on our own initiative. It is an individual, personal expression of commitment, yes. But it is commitment within a community, invited by a community, approved and supported by a community. This is expressed ritually in both Baptism and Confirmation.

And it is, if we are mature enough to accept it as that, the community "sending us off" in mission. The community is recognizing that God has "set apart" each one of us "for the work to which" he has called each one. We are consecrated by Baptism to do the work of Jesus *Prophet, Priest,* and *King*. At home. At work. In family and social life. In business and politics. Each one of us is "set apart" for the work to which God has called us. The *Presentation of Gifts* invites us to *remember* and *reaffirm* that as there are many hosts but one bread, we are many members but one body, with many gifts but one goal. We live to make God known and loved: *"O God, let all the nations praise you."*

In **John 12:44-50** Jesus said, "Who sees me sees him who sent me." We need to be conscious that who sees us sees the Church. And Jesus. People will judge both by what they see in us, for better or worse. Let it be *prophetic witness.*

Decision: Know you are "set apart" as one of many, to be a witness.

MAY 19, 2011

The *Responsorial* (*Psalm* 89) affirms God's faithfulness and "steadfast love," even when we are unfaithful and he appears to have forgotten us: *"Forever I will sing the goodness of the Lord."*

In **Acts 13:13-25** Paul reminds his hearers they are a chosen people, and that God has "made this people great" by guiding their history through chosen individuals, some of whom sinned and betrayed him: "The God of this people chose our ancestors...." He mentions the judges, the prophet Samuel, and the kings Saul and David, about whom "God testified, 'I have found David... to be a man after my own heart, who will fulfill my every wish.'"

We need to remember that David was a rapist who betrayed and murdered a loyal officer to cover up his crime. God punished him for that, but did not withdraw his love or the promises he made to David. Does that say something about his fidelity to us?[1]

When Paul reminds us of the great things God has done and is doing through his people, do we choose to be part of it? At every Mass the *Presentation of Gifts* invites us to make or reaffirm that choice. We hear the Lord saying, "Whom shall I send?" And we are called to respond: "Here am I; send me!" Under the symbols of bread and wine we place our own bodies and blood on the altar as a "living sacrifice to God." We present our bodies, as Mary did, to be the Body of Christ: "Here am I... let it be with me according to your word.... This is my body, given for you."[2]

In **John 13:16-20** Jesus makes clear that betrayal by his chosen ones does not mean he was deceived: "I know the kind of men I chose." He told them ahead of time about Judas "so that when it takes place you may believe that I AM" (that is, God: *Exodus* 3:13-15). Judas was a good choice. But he had free will and sinned. If he had repented like Peter he could have been as great as any of the Twelve. Jesus would have stood by the call he gave him.

He extended this: "I tell you, whoever accepts one whom I send accepts me; and... accepts him who sent me." Unfaithful ministers, whether laity or clergy, bishops or popes, are not a reason to reject Jesus or the Church—or even the ministers themselves, if they repent. The danger they are to others may exclude some from ministry, as all child abusers must be excluded absolutely. But we do not exclude them from the Church or from our love. Once they have "turned back" like David and Peter, their sin is "taken away."[3]

At Baptism all of us "presented our bodies as a living sacrifice," and promised not to be "conformed to this world." But we all fail. So at every Mass, in the *Presentation of Gifts* we present ourselves again. And are accepted.[4]

[1] *2Samuel* 11:1 to 12:27. In 1Samuel 13:14 God calls David "a man after his own heart." Read *Psalm* 89.
[2] *Isaiah* 6:8. See *Luke* 1:38; 22:19; *Romans* 12:1-2; *Hebrews* 2:13; 10:5-7.
[3] *Luke* 22:31-34.
[4] *Romans* 12:1-2.

Decision: See God's fidelity also, whenever you see your own or others' sins.

MAY 20, 2011

The *Responsorial* (*Psalm* 2) recalls what God said of Jesus at his baptism and Transfiguration: *"You are my Son; this day I have begotten you."* Jesus is not just a prophet; he is the divine Son of God. This gives special meaning to the Father's words, *"Listen to him."*[1]

Peter announces in **Acts 13:26-33**: "We bring you the good news that what God promised to our ancestors he has fulfilled for us… by raising Jesus." But his point follows in verses 40-41:

> Beware, that what the prophets said does not happen to you: "Look, you scoffers! Be amazed and perish, for in your days I am doing a work, a work that you will never believe, even if someone tells you."

If God said of Jesus, *"You are my Son…,"* the news about him is not something to take lightly.

It is arguable whether the worst response to the Good News is to deny it by refusing to believe, or just to ignore it by refusing to take a stand. Only once do the Gospels say Jesus was "angry." He had asked the Pharisees a question and they were "silent." Just refused to answer. Jesus "looked around at them with anger… grieved at their hardness of heart." If they had answered, even with the wrong answer, he could have argued with them and perhaps convinced them. But there is no way to communicate with stone silence.[2]

This may not be as rare as we think. How many people, even among those in church, have never taken a deep, conscious, personal stand toward the Good News of Jesus Christ? We think first of the youth, of course: those who are present at Mass but obviously not participating in any personal way. They aren't denying anything they have been taught or anything their parents believe—not yet—but they are just not getting involved in it. They are inside of the church but outside of the action. They have not really taken a stand yet toward the Good News. Or toward Jesus. Or toward what is going on in the Mass. (It is all the same thing). They may not even be aware of it. Dangerous.

How many adults are almost as uninvolved? Many may have made the decision to keep "going to Mass," and "obeying the rules" in the Church, but without giving to Jesus Christ the kind of total, personal, all-embracing response God called for when he said, "This is my Son… listen to him!"

That is why every Mass, during the *Presentation of Gifts*, invites us to recommit, to declare ourselves personally and publicly by sending up a host that represents us to be placed on the altar as a sign of our response to the Good News. It is an important moment; not one to take lightly.

In **John 14:1-6** Jesus says, "Believe in God, believe also in me." Or "Trust in God; trust in me." In practice, we reveal (and experience) our real faith by where we place our trust. If we really believe Jesus is "the Way, and the Truth, and the Life" we will be serious about learning his truth and following his way. If not, we don't really want his Life.

[1]*Matthew* 3:13-17; 17:1-5.
[2]*Mark* 3:1-5.

Decision: Declare yourself. Come alive during the *Presentation of Gifts.*

MAY 21, 2011

The *Responsorial* (*Psalm* 98) declares: "*All the ends of the earth have seen the saving power of God.*" Have you?

The *Presentation of Gifts* is a turning-point in the Mass. It marks the transition, not only from the *Liturgy of the Word* to the *Liturgy of the Eucharist*, but also from what could be an understanding of the Mass that is merely human to a realization of the divine mystery that is taking place.

A flight attendant said to a priest on a plane, "I have been to the Catholic Mass. I'm with you through the Scripture readings and preaching; but after that you go into all that mumbo-jumbo and you lose me." Good insight.

Nothing from the *Presentation of Gifts* on makes any sense unless we understand the mystery that Jesus is being made present on the altar in flesh and blood. And that we are present in him. That when Jesus died we died in him and rose in him as his body endowed with the divine life of God. That in him we are a "new creation." Made divine. Having "become Christ."

That is the mystery we begin to express when we put ourselves on the altar with the bread and wine to be offered: our flesh in Christ for the life of the world.[1]

The strange statement Paul makes in **Acts 13:44-52** applies to many believers: "...since you do not think yourselves worthy of eternal life..." We can believe in *everlasting* life, because that could be just human life extended. But only God

has *eternal* life: life without beginning or end. And we balk at admitting we actually share in the divine life of God. We "do not think ourselves worthy" to say we have "become Christ." To say we are "divine" is too much to accept.

If we do not accept it, we are failing in faith. And from the *Presentation of Gifts* on, much of the Mass will be just "mumbo-jumbo" to us.

But if we can put ordinary bread on the altar and believe God transforms that bread into Christ's real Body and Blood, why do we balk at saying he can take humans, made in his image and likeness, and make us his true body by sharing his divine life with us? True, we remain our human selves (while the bread ceases to be bread), but we acquire the added identity of Christ himself through union with him. Christ lives and acts, not only *with* us but *in* us and *through* us.[2]

In **John 14:7-14** Jesus says, "Whoever has seen me has seen the Father." When you act by grace, would you say, "Who sees me sees Jesus?" Hears his voice? Experiences his love? Do you believe Jesus can do in and through your body things as great as he did in the body he had on earth? Was Jesus exaggerating when he said, "Whoever believes in me will do the works that I do, *and will do greater ones than these*"? Believe—so that "*All the ends of the earth may see the saving power of God.*"

[1] *John* 6:51; *1Corinthians* 1:24; *2Corinthians* 4:8-11.
[2] See *Galatians* 2:20; *Colossians* 2:6; *Romans* 12:1-5; *1Corinthians* 12:1-27; *Ephesians* 3:1 to 4:24.

Decision: Take Christ at his word. Believe he acts *with* you, *in* you, *through* you.

FOR REFLECTION AND DISCUSSION:
EASTER WEEK FOUR

The Fourth Week of Easter: Jesus is leading us somewhere. To be a Christian is to *move*, to follow the shepherd who died and rose to lead us out of enslavement to a corrupt and corrupting society into divine life.

Invitation: Follow the "beaten path" only when the Spirit shows it is on course. Whatever is proposed to us, we should ask whether the basic motivation for it is grounded in values taught by Jesus.

Ask yourself in prayer and others in discussion: How could the statements below make Mass mean more if we stay aware of them during Mass?

Acts 11:1-18: We develop into *prophets* when we learn to look to laws' goal, and respond to the mind of God behind them. This is our passage into maturity.

We express this in the *Presentation of Gifts* when we present ourselves to be transformed as the bread we present will be "transformed" into the "Bread of life."

Acts 11:19-26: The *Presentation of Gifts* invites us to embrace *our messianic anointing*. We "go up" symbolically with the bread and wine to re-commit to *witness* as prophets, *ministry* as priests, and *leadership* as stewards of his kingship.

Acts 12:24 to 13:5: In the *Presentation of Gifts* we express our individual, personal commitment, but as invited, approved, and supported *by* and *within a community*.

The *Presentation of Gifts* invites us to *remember* that as there are many hosts but one bread, we are many members but all one body; with many gifts but one goal.

Acts 13:13-25: The *Presentation of Gifts* invites us to respond to Christ's call in spite of our sins, saying: "Here am I; send me!" We all fail, so we keep presenting ourselves again at every Mass. And are always accepted.

Acts 13:26-33: Is it worse to deny the Good News by refusing to believe, or to accept it without taking a conscious, personal stand? Every *Presentation of Gifts* invites us to declare ourselves personally and publicly. It is an important moment.

Acts 13:44-52: The *Presentation of Gifts* is a turning-point in the Mass, marking a transition from the *Liturgy of the Word* to the *Liturgy of the Eucharist*, and from an understanding of the Mass that could be merely human to a realization of the divine mystery that is taking place: Jesus being made present on the altar and we in him.

Decisions:

Be conscious you are moving. Keep looking ahead to see where you are going, and back to see where you have been.
Focus on Jesus. Use the "WIT" prayer all day long.
Ask if you have reason to be glad you are Christian. If so, express it.
Know you are "set apart" from this world, as one of many, to be a witness.
See God's fidelity also, whenever you see your own or others' sins.
Declare yourself. Come alive during the Presentation of Gifts
Take Christ at his word. Believe he acts *with* you, *in* you, *through* you.

May 22, 2011
Light and Life through Conscious Union with Jesus

Inventory

The *Entrance Antiphon* invites us: *"Sing to the Lord"* because he has *"done marvelous deeds"* and *"revealed his saving power"* (*Psalm* 97). What "marvelous deeds" of God have I experienced? How do I see his "saving power" revealed in the Church and in the world today?

Input

In the *Opening Prayer* we profess our belief that the Father is "looking upon us with love" and giving us "true freedom." This is not just *freedom from* enslaving attitudes and values, but *freedom to* make *personal choices* that "bring us to the inheritance" God has promised. Our free, personal, creative, innovative choices in response to God's word can be life-giving and reveal God's "saving power" because the Spirit is given to us to inspire them. The *readings* show this happening.

Hear the Spirit:

The *Responsorial* (*Psalm* 33) teaches us that the choice to *trust* in God, expecting to experience his guidance within us, opens the way to his saving graces: *"Lord, let your mercy be upon us, as we place our trust in you."*

Acts 6:1-7 shows the Holy Spirit guiding the community in response to unforeseen challenges that arise in their life as Church. Cultural differences threatened to cause division between the Greek-speaking "Hellenist" Christians and those of Hebrew origin. The Twelve met with all the disciples and made a proposal "acceptable to the whole community." It was to select seven men "filled with the Spirit and wisdom" (the names show they were all Greek) to deal with the Hellenists' needs. These men they "presented to the apostles, who prayed and laid hands on them." The report ends, "The word of God continued to spread, and the number of disciples increased greatly." By praying and discerning together as a community, the Church had courage to take decisive action, and experienced that God's *"mercy"* was indeed *"upon them,"* since they *"placed their trust in him."*

A Living Structure

1Peter 2:4-9 invites the disciples to let themselves be formed into a structured community—"be built into a spiritual house"—but one made of "living stones," with Jesus, also "a living stone," as its cornerstone. People sometimes speak disparagingly of "organized religion." But an "unorganized religion" cannot really be a church (an "assembly" with identity). The Church does not exist apart from the "organizational Church," any more than a body can exist apart from its skeleton. But we don't *reduce* the Church to its organizational structure, any more than we reduce the body to its bones. For the Church to be authentic, the stones of its structure must be *alive*.

Jesus, the "living stone" must be the "cornerstone." The Church is alive through her connection to the living person of Jesus. The Church is alive because her members have "become Christ" by Baptism, dying to their isolated, individual human lives and rising "in Christ" to live as parts in a whole, members of the body of Christ, and to *"grow up in every way into him who is the head*, into Christ, from whom the whole body, *joined and knit together... as each part is working properly, promotes the body's growth in *building itself up in love"* (*Ephesians* 4: 15-16). The "organizational Church" is, in reality, a living, growing, mutually supportive, organized community continuing to carry out the mission of Jesus Prophet, Priest, and King. We are consecrated to "proclaim the mighty acts of him who called us out of darkness into his marvelous light." For this we need to keep ourselves always aware of Christ, refer every experience to him, and base all our decisions solidly on him, the cornerstone.

WAY, TRUTH, AND LIFE

John 14:1-12 gives us a basis for praying, *"Lord, let your mercy be upon us,* *as we place our trust in you."* Jesus himself said, "Do not let your hearts be troubled. You have faith in God, have faith also in me." Jesus is not just a teacher from the past, to use like a reference book and imitate as best we can. He did not just teach us some truths and point out some directions. Jesus *is* "the way, and the truth, and the life." He is Truth enlightening our minds now from within. He himself *is* the Way. To follow his way is to live in him. The way is not something he points out; it is something we find through deep, conscious, personal union with him as his body on earth. We know the way only by knowing Jesus. We follow the way only by *being* Jesus.

The fact is, Jesus is the Way and the Truth for us by being our Life. Because he lives in us and shares his life with us, we see truth by his light and walk by his strength. This explains his shocking statement: "Whoever believes in me will do the works I do and *greater ones* than these." He said, "the Father who dwells in me is doing his works." And it is Jesus dwelling in us who, in each one of us, can do things he could not do in or through any other human body, including the one he received from Mary. He is our Life; we are his body. In combination, we are the mystery of the risen Jesus living and acting on earth.

INSIGHT
When have I seen Christ's "saving power" revealed in my actions? In the life of the Church? What can I do that is "greater than" what Jesus did?

INITIATIVE
Put your trust in Jesus dwelling and working within you, and have the courage to make decisions based on his truth that depend on his strength.

MAY 23, 2011

The *Responsorial* (*Psalm* 115) teaches us to look for the real cause of the wonders we experience: *"Not to us, O LORD, but to your name give glory."*

In **Acts 14:5-18** Paul and Barnabas restore a man to the level of health and being that most humans are born with. Healing the cripple was a miracle, but the same thing could have been accomplished, conceivably, at least, by sufficiently advanced medical technology when he was born. When the crowd proclaimed them gods for it, Paul and Barnabas tried to focus them on the miracle right before their eyes that they were ignoring: on what no god, but only God as Source of being itself can do:

> You should turn from these empty idols to the living God, who made heaven and earth and the sea and all these hold.... giving you rain from heaven... filling you with food and your hearts with joy.

There is something Paul did not point out, though: if the crowd thought Paul and Barnabas were gods because they restored the cripple to ordinary human health, what should they have taken them for if they had realized that these men, through their ministry, had the power to give them divine life, life on the level of God? To make them sharers in the life of God himself?

A good doctor can bring our human health up to par. A good teacher can enable us to understand any truth available to human reason. With sufficient goodwill we can reach the level of heroic human love. And we can legitimately hope and strive for any good and happiness available on earth. But only Jesus Christ, and those in and through whom he acts as his body on earth, can give divine life. The power to understand Truth accessible only to God. The "perfection of Love" proper to God alone. A happiness no one but God can dream of. This is what Paul offered:

> I pray that... you may have the power to comprehend, with all the saints, what is the breadth and length and height and depth, and to know the love of Christ that surpasses knowledge, so that you may be filled with all the fullness of God. Now to him who by the power at work within us is able to accomplish abundantly far more than all we can ask or imagine, to him be glory in the church and in Christ Jesus to all generations.[1]

This is the glorious ministry for which we offer ourselves at Baptism. It is to this that we recommit ourselves at the *Presentation of Gifts* when we put our human selves on the altar as bread—"fruit of the earth and work of human hands"—to be offered and given in Christ for the life of the world.

John 14:21-26 responds to our fear to believe this is possible. The same John who wrote: "No one has ever seen God," reports Jesus as saying, "Whoever has seen me has seen the Father... Those who love me will be loved by my Father, and I will love them and *reveal myself to them.*" More than that, "We will come to them and *make our home* with them." John repeats it: "If we love one another, God *lives in us,* and his love is perfected in us." Ponder that. Then say, *"Not to us, O LORD, but to your name give glory."*[2]

[1]*Ephesians* 3:16-21.
[2]*John* 14:9; *1John* 4:12-16.

> **Decision: Accept the miracle** of your being, both human and divine. Use it.

MAY 24, 2011

The *Responsorial* (*Psalm* 145) reminds us what we are by Baptism and what we are called and consecrated to do: "*Your friends make known, O Lord, the glorious splendor of your kingdom.*"

Acts 14:19-28 shows us the pattern of early evangelization: 1. Inspired by the Holy Spirit "while they were worshiping the Lord and fasting," the whole Christian community "laid their hands on Paul and Barnabas and sent them off." 2. Those sent preached and made converts. 3. In each of the churches before they left they "appointed *presbyters* (elders) for them, and, with prayer and fasting, entrusted them to the Lord in whom they had put their faith." This was to assure the continuance of the new communities. 4. On their return, those sent "called the church together and gave an account of what God had done with them."

The word "elders" is the correct word for those we call priests. Grammatically, the word "priest" comes from *presbyteros* (elder) in Greek, which became *prêtre* in French and *Priester* in German. But through mistaken usage, the meaning actually changed to what the Latin *sacerdos* designates: a "sacred" person (*sacer*) ordained to perform sacred acts. Compare this to the Greek *hieros*, meaning "priest" or "keeper of the sacred," from which "hierarchy" comes.

The bishops at the second Vatican Council (1962-1965) attempted to restore the authentic terminology. They tried to reserve the word "priest" (in Latin *sacerdos*) for *Jesus alone* and for all who became "priests in the Priest" by "becoming Christ" at Baptism. For ordained clergy they used the word *presbyter*. But the translators defeated their purpose by carelessly translating both words as "priest" in English.[1]

As a result, most Catholics have no understanding of their baptismal anointing as "priests." When we say during the *Presentation of Gifts,* to the "elder" presiding at Mass, "May the Lord accept the sacrifice at your hands…" we are not thinking of ourselves as priests offering the sacrifice equally with the presider. We think of him as the priest, of him as offering the sacrifice, and of ourselves as the community he is doing it *for* more than *with*. Progress has been made in correcting this error, but not yet enough.

In **John 14:27-31**, Jesus showed us the way to peace is *surrender*: "My peace I give to you…. Do not let your hearts be troubled or afraid… I love the Father… and I am doing exactly what the Father told me," We send ourselves up under the form of bread to be placed on the altar in an act of surrendering our bodies, minds, hearts, and lives to be joined to Christ and offered with him. We abandon ourselves to the Father's will, both in life and in death. There is no greater security, no greater peace. "*Your friends make known, O Lord, the glorious splendor of your kingdom.*"

[1]See *Hebrews*, chapters 7-10, and Patrick Dunne, now Bishop of Auckland, New Zealand: *Priesthood: A Re-examination of the Roman Catholic Theology of the Presbyterate*, Alba House, 1990, p. 110.

Decision: Find yourself by losing yourself in the *Presentation of Gifts.*

MAY 25, 2011

The *Responsorial* (*Psalm* 122) identifies authentic religion with joy: *"Let us go rejoicing to the house of the Lord."* But some people try to make happiness consist in something that cannot give happiness—*law observance*—and call it salvation. This is Phariseeism.

In **Acts 15:1-6**, when Paul and Barnabas "reported the conversion of the Gentiles, [they] brought great joy to all the believers." Well, not to all. "Some believers who belonged to the sect of the Pharisees stood up and said, 'It is necessary for them to be ordered to keep the law of Moses... Unless you are circumcised you cannot be saved.'"

Faith was not enough. Loving God was not enough. Keeping the Ten Commandments was not enough. Even keeping the New Law of Jesus in the "Sermon on the Mount" was not enough. Evidence of having received the divine life of God and the "gift of the Spirit" was not enough. To be saved you had to keep all the rules and observances that made up Jewish religious culture: circumcision, eating kosher food, observing the minute rules of Sabbath observance, etc., etc.

The Catholic equivalent is, or at one time was, abstaining from meat on Fridays, fasting during Lent and for a set time before Communion, never touching the host or even the chalice with your fingers if you were a lay person, going to Mass every Sunday, having your marriage witnessed by a priest or deacon, accepting celibacy as a condition for ordination as a presbyter, wearing a Roman collar if you were a presbyter and, if you were a woman, a hat in church (and *never* entering the sanctuary during Mass!), making your "Easter duty" by annual Confession and Communion—all Church rules and none of them, in themselves, necessary for salvation. None of these rules was obligatory from the beginning. Others were, such as the rule that women should not come to church "with their hair braided, or with gold, pearls, or expensive clothes... not teach or speak in church," and that bishops should be "married only once" and "keep their children submissive and respectful in every way." Such rules can, do, and should change with the times. We do not (repeat: do *not*) say we should not keep them; just that keeping them must never be identified with "salvation."[1]

John 15:1-8 tells us what salvation is: being one with Jesus as branches are one with the vine, sharing in his life. That is why we do not stop after hearing the words—and the laws—of God in the *Liturgy of the Word* but go on to "present our bodies" in the *Presentation of Gifts* as a "living sacrifice" to be offered with and in Christ during the *Eucharistic Prayer.*[2] We give our lives to live his life, knowing that "apart from him" we can do nothing. For this we *"go rejoicing to the house of the Lord."*

[1] *1Timothy* 2:9 to 3:4; *1Corinthians* 11:4-15; 14:34-35; *1Peter* 3:3.
[2] *Romans* 12:1-2.

Decision: Be a prophet. Hear God's words as words of life, not just law.

MAY 26, 2011

The *Responsorial* (*Psalm* 96) says, *"Proclaim God's marvelous deeds to all the nations."*

What do we proclaim? In the Mass, during the *Introductory Rites* we proclaim the Good News in a brief résumé of the early "kerygmatic" or "heralding" preaching. This is *evangelization*. Then in the *Liturgy of the Word* we proclaim the "word of God" more extensively, to nurture and encourage *discipleship*. But a temptation enters here: the natural human tendency to reduce God's word to moral teachings, to instructions on how to live. Even though based on the teachings and example of Jesus, this can degenerate into a religion of law-observance, in which, for practical purposes, what we do and don't do is really all that counts.

Before we go beyond this, however, as we must, we should read *Psalm* 119:

> Happy are those whose way is blameless, who walk in the law of the LORD... who keep his decrees, who seek him with their whole heart, who also do no wrong, but walk in his ways.

Does this Psalm contradict yesterday's reflection by saying happiness is found in keeping God's law? No. Not if we notice phrases like "With my *whole heart I seek you*;" "I will *praise you*... when I learn," "*Make me understand*..." "Let your *steadfast love come to me*..." "The *LORD is my portion*..." "*You are good and do good; teach me*..." "*I am yours; save me*," "*preserve my life* according to your *steadfast love*." In this psalm, law-observance is a means to *know God*, to

understand his heart and ways, to enter into the life he alone can give. Likewise, in the Mass, God's *words* prepare us to enter into *life*—not through good behavior, but through *union* with God in grace.

In **Acts 15:7-21**, the Church decided not to impose Jewish law on the Gentile converts. James said, "For generations past, Moses has been read aloud every Sabbath in the synagogues." He agreed with Peter that we need more. We are saved, not just by hearing God's word, or even by basing our human conduct on it, but "through the grace of the Lord Jesus." All the hymns, prayers, reading, and preaching of the *Liturgy of the Word* are to prepare us for the *mystery* to which we surrender ourselves in the *Liturgy of the Eucharist*, beginning with the *Presentation of Gifts*.

In **John 15:9-11** Jesus says the reason to keep his law is to abide in his love: *"If you keep my commandments, you will abide in my love."* This means to live in him as branches in the vine, sharing his divine life. To share in his own act of knowing by the gift of faith. To share in his own act of loving by the gift of divine love. To share in his own intentions, dreams, goals, and desires by the gift of divine hope. It means to *"become Christ"* by Baptism and the "grace of our Lord Jesus Christ," which is the "favor of sharing in God's divine life."

"I have said these things to you so that my joy may be in you, and that your joy may be complete." The joy of religion is not in the sense of security law-observance gives, but in the *life* of union with others and with God "in Christ."

Decision: Go beyond God's words to God's Word. Present yourself to *be Christ*.

MAY 27, 2011

The *Responsorial* (*Psalm* 57) reminds us we pray as a community: "*I will give you thanks among the peoples, O Lord.*"

Acts 15:22-31 shows us the Church's response to the division caused by those who "without any mandate from us have upset you with their teachings and disturbed your peace of mind." See the beginning of this chapter: "Certain individuals came down from Judea and were teaching the brothers, 'Unless you are circumcised according to the custom of Moses, you cannot be saved.'"

This raises the question of good and bad prophets. Everyone has the right—and the obligation—to speak up within the community (parish, diocese, family, and friends) and to say whatever God inspires for the good of the Church:

> This Synod [the Second Vatican Council] urges all concerned to work hard to prevent or correct any abuses, excesses, or defects which may have crept in here or there, and to restore all things to a more ample praise of Christ and of God.[1]

How do we know what is inspired by God? The ultimate answer is "by discernment of spirits": an art, not a science, and a gift of God rather than a human talent. There are guidelines, but we can begin by distinguishing "prophets" from "Pharisees."[2]

Prophets can summon to law-observance, but typically do it with insight into the deeper, spiritual purpose of the law and into the real damage non-observance causes. Pharisees just call for literal conformity, and recognize no damage

but the fact alone that the law is not being kept. Those arguing for circumcision were not seeing the deep meaning this symbol had (surpassed by Baptism). The only evil they weighed against the good of so many conversions was just the fact of non-conformity. The same spirit moves those in the Church today (jokingly referred to as the "liturgical police") who scrutinize their pastors and report to the bishop any departure from the letter of liturgical instructions. They don't understand that their pastors are obeying Vatican II:

> Pastors of souls must realize that, when the liturgy is celebrated, *more is required* than the mere observance of the laws governing valid and licit celebration. It is *their duty also to ensure* that the faithful take part *knowingly, actively, and fruitfully.*[3]

The pastor who "knows his sheep" has the right and obligation to make the adjustments required to do this. Pharisees criticize, not damage; only supposed disobedience.

John 15:12-17 Jesus said, "I no longer call you *servants*... but *friends*, because *I have made known to you* everything that I have heard from my Father." Those who know the Lord interpret rules according to his mind and heart as expressed to Peter: "If you love me, *feed my sheep.*" Pastors sometime suffer from those who "do not care for the sheep," but only for laws. The "good shepherd" risks this, and Jesus says there is "no greater love."[4]

[1] Vatican II: *The Church*, no. 51.
[2] See *The Spiritual Exercises of St. Ignatius of Loyola*, nos. 313-336.
[3] "Sacred Liturgy," no. 11.
[4] See *John* 10:11-15; 21:15-17.

Decision: Interpret all laws according to the mind and heart of Christ.

MAY 28, 2011

The *Responsorial* (*Psalm* 100) is: *"Let all the earth cry out to God with joy."*

Yesterday Jesus said, "No one has greater love than this, to lay down one's life for one's friends." In today's reading from **Acts 16:1-10** we see Timothy, not laying down his life, but literally shedding his blood in circumcision for no other reason than to keep local prejudice from being an obstacle to the gift of life he and Paul were offering. Paul, who insisted that the law of circumcision was abolished, nevertheless "had him circumcised because of the Jews of that region." Love is the most demanding law.[1]

The Scripture readings and homily in the *Liturgy of the Word* at Mass can cause division. People have different opinions, influenced by personal leaning toward the left or the right. So what keeps the *Liturgy of the Word* from splitting us into separate camps of "conservatives" and "liberals" who show more partisan allegiance than "communion in the Holy Spirit"?

First, as soon as the readings and homily are over, we express our unified agreement on the "rock bottom" doctrines of the *Profession of Faith*. Then we pray together, united in love, for the needs enumerated in the *General Intercessions* (*Prayer of the Faithful*). These have a definite unifying effect. As we hear what the community prays for, it makes us proud to be part of it.

But we go beyond this in the *Presentation of Gifts*. Now everyone in the church passes from words to action, from partisan consciousness to deep awareness of mystical union with each other in the "one bread" which the bread we place on the altar is about to become as the one Body of Christ.

> Because there is one bread, we who are many are one body, for we all partake of the one bread.[2]

Everyone is sending up a host on the same plate, brought up from the back of church, through the whole congregation, to show that the whole community is offering itself together, not just as isolated individuals. And all are being placed on the altar in re-affirmation of the Baptism in which all "presented their bodies as a living sacrifice to God." All differences and personal preferences are swallowed up in one communal surrender of ourselves, body, mind, heart, and will, to *be Christ* and live as Christ for the life of the world. In the *Presentation of Gifts* we are all committing to this together.

The *Presentation of Gifts* reminds us of **John 15:18-21**: "You do not belong to the world, but I have chosen you out of the world...." Through our human natures we are bread of this earth; people whom "earth has given and human hands have made"—products of our parents' flesh, formed by our human choices. But "in Christ" we are one with the Bread of Life that transcends this world. Our call as *prophets* is to be the "leaven" that lifts up the world through a lifestyle inexplicable without grace.[3]

[1] *Romans* 2:25-29; *Galatians* 5:6, 6:15.
[2] *1Corinthians* 10:17.
[3] *Matthew* 13:33.

Decision: Lose all and find all by offering yourself as one with all.

FOR REFLECTION AND DISCUSSION: EASTER WEEK FIVE

The Fifth Week of Easter: By discerning together, the Church shows trust and receives courage to take decisive action. The Church is a *community*: organized and kept alive through awareness of the "cornerstone," the living person of Jesus.

Invitation: Choose to *trust* in God, expecting to experience his guidance.

Ask yourself in prayer and others in discussion: How could the statements below make Mass mean more if we stay aware of them during Mass?

Acts 14:5-18: In the *Presentation of Gifts* we don't ask God to make the gifts better bread and wine, but to change them into the "Bread of life" and "spiritual drink." This reminds us that to bear witness to the "grace of our Lord Jesus Christ" it is not enough to live a better human life. We must live clearly by the life of God.

Acts 14:19-28: When we say, "May the Lord accept the sacrifice at your hands…" we affirm we are priests offering the sacrifice equally with the presider.

John 14:27-31: At the *Presentation of Gifts* we surrender our bodies to be joined to Christ and offered with him—to death and life—during the *Eucharistic Prayer*.

Acts 15:1-6: What "brought great joy to all the believers" was the *conversion* of the Gentiles, not their conformity to Jewish rules. Keeping the Catholic equivalent of such rules is good, but is not "salvation." We "present our bodies as a living sacrifice" to live by a new life, which must not be identified with old laws.

Acts 15:7-21: All the hymns, prayers, readings, and preaching of the *Liturgy of the Word* should prepare us for the *mystery* to which we surrender ourselves in the *Liturgy of the Eucharist*, beginning with the *Presentation of Gifts*.

Acts 15:22-31: Prophets summon to law-observance with insight into the deeper, spiritual purpose of the law, pointing out the real damage non-observance causes. Pharisees ignore both, calling for literal conformity for conformity's sake.

Acts 16:1-10: The Scripture readings and homily in the *Liturgy of the Word* at Mass might cause division. But we go beyond this in the *Presentation of Gifts*, when all differences are swallowed up in a communal surrender to be one "in Christ" as the one "Bread of Life" that transcends this world.

Decisions:

Put your trust in Jesus dwelling and working within you. Have courage.
Depend on the Spirit. Base decisions on his truth. Rely on his strength.
Accept the miracle of your being, both human and divine. Use it.
Find yourself by losing yourself in the *Presentation of Gifts*.
Be a prophet. Seek guidance through God's words, not just laws.
Go beyond God's words to God's Word. Present yourself to *be Christ*.
Interpret all laws according to the mind and heart of Christ.
Offer yourself to lose all in order to find all, be one with all.

May 29, 2011
Spirit of Christ, Spirit of Joy and Peace

INVENTORY

What gives me my greatest joy in life right now? What liberation, healing, or empowerment in my life can I attribute to the fact that Jesus is risen from the dead?

INPUT

Everything in the liturgy is speaking to us of joy. The *Entrance Antiphon*: "Speak out with a voice of joy…." The *Opening Prayer*: "God, help us to celebrate our joy…." The *Responsorial* (*Psalm* 66): "*Let all the earth cry out to God with joy.*" Why? Because of the awesome power God has used for us; because by "the resurrection… the Lord has set his people free"; because at the preaching of the Good News "many possessed, paralyzed, or lame were cured."

THE GIFT OF THE SPIRIT

In **Acts 8:5-17** the crown of conversion is the *gift of the Holy Spirit*. In Luke's Gospel the Holy Spirit brings about the conception of Jesus in Mary's womb, and this gift distinguishes the baptism of John the Baptizer from the Baptism Jesus gives. In John's Gospel Jesus declares that no one enters into the kingdom of heaven without it, the Spirit is the Father's great gift to those who believe, and the gift of the Spirit is the fruit of Jesus' resurrection. It empowers the Church to continue his mission and to forgive sins. In *Acts* the Spirit gives power to proclaim the Good News to the whole world and to bear witness to Jesus as prophets.

In Paul's letters receiving the Spirit was proof of faith and was revealed in joy; a joy "in the Holy Spirit" that, together with hope, love, and peace is a characteristic of the kingdom, even in time of persecution. To make his case against the legalists, Paul appeals to the Galatians' experience of receiving the Holy Spirit. Clearly, a conscious, experienced *joy in the Spirit* is a constitutive element of true Christian life. It should lead us to sing, "*Let all the earth cry out to God with joy.*"[1]

PLEDGE OF LIFE:

1Peter 3:15-18 tells us, "Always be ready to make your defense to anyone who demands from you an accounting for the hope that is in you." If we live as *prophets*—that is, in a way that does not make sense without the Gospel—then obviously we have set our hearts on something beyond what this world promises. When our lifestyle or behavior raises the question of what that is, we should be ready to answer. Not just with abstract truths or doctrines of faith, but in some way out of our *experience*. The joy of experiencing the Holy Spirit empowering us from within is such an experience.

Remember, St. Paul based his argument against legalism on the Galatians' experience of the Holy Spirit.

He didn't argue *to* that experience; he argued *from* it (*Galatians* 3:2-5). In the same way, we should be able to base our hope of resurrection on our *experience* of living here and now by the Spirit of God.

We are not speaking about strange and "mystical" experiences: overwhelming feelings and inexplicable sensations. No, we are talking about *choices* that we experience ourselves making, and making with confidence and courage, when no merely human knowledge or experience would justify them—choices based on faith; choices based on trust in God's promises; choices that are clearly options to love God more than anything on this earth. These choices don't necessarily give us *feelings* of absolute certitude, or of fearless confidence, or even of passionate devotion. It is just that the choices cannot be explained unless their foundation is a graced (divine) *certitude, confidence,* and *devotion*—whether these are felt or present to us mostly by an aching awareness of their absence! We *know* we believe, trust, and love because we find ourselves *acting* out of faith, hope, and love. We experience the Holy Spirit as the "condition for the possibility" of the way we are choosing to live. And deep down, deeper than both feelings and conscious, rational thought, we *know* we are living in truth and love. We experience even

more certitude when persecution, dryness, and doubts take away all human motivation for living the Christian life. In the absence of the human we are confirmed in our experience of the divine.

"You Know Him..."

In **John 14:15-21** Jesus not only promises to send the Spirit into our hearts; he also tells us what the fruit of his presence is: "You *know* him, because he abides with you, and he will be in you.... You will see me. Because I live, you also will live. On that day you will *know* that I am in my Father, and you in me, and I in you." This is the source of our joy.

He promises we will experience in some way all Three Persons: Father, Son, and Spirit. How? By *loving*: "Those who love me will be loved by my Father, and I will love them and reveal myself to them." In the act of loving God we experience being loved. Those who choose to live in love will experience God loving in them. And they will join their voices to those who sing: "*Let all the earth cry out to God with joy.*"

[1]*Luke* 1:35; 3:16; *John* 3:5; 14:16; 20:19-23; *Acts* 1:8; 2:17-18; 10:47; 13:52; *Romans* 14:17; 15:13; *Galatians* 3:2-5; 5:22; *1 Thessalonians* 1:6.

INSIGHT
Is it not true that I experience my faith, not just as an opinion, and not just as something I was taught, but as something I know—even when I feel doubts?

INITIATIVE
Let the Spirit move you to find your joy in loving. Consciously do everything you do out of love for God and people.

May 30, 2011

The *Responsorial* (*Psalm* 149) tells us, *"The Lord takes delight in his people."* Surprised? Many of us may be inclined to think he just puts up with us!

We could wonder what to meditate on in **Acts 16:11-15.** All it seems to say is that Paul and his companions went to Philippi in Macedonia, part of modern Greece, to evangelize. They went down to the river to pray (and probably have a picnic), struck up a conversation with some women gathered there, and made an impression on Lydia, who said "If you are convinced that I believe in the Lord, come and stay at my home." And they did. This was the first time Paul preached in Europe.

What this passage does is show the apostles (and God?) in what we might call a relaxed moment. Lydia liked the apostles; they liked her; they went to her house. What attracted them? The fact she believed. What makes God "take delight" in us? Many things. But a major one is just the fact we believe. Jesus told his disciples, "the Father himself loves you, because you have loved me and *have believed* that I came from God." And before that: "Those who love me will keep my word, and my Father will love them, and *we will come to them and make our home with them.*"[1]

A good reason to *express* our faith and love is so we ourselves will be "convinced that we believe in the Lord." Believe personally. Consciously. Deliberately. Firmly. And love him.

It really helps if we do this consciously at Mass, meaning all the words we say. In the *Presentation of Gifts* we should see a connection between our giving a host to Christ as an expression of our love and him giving a host to us in Communion as an expression of his.

In **John 15:26 to 16:4** Jesus says the way we know we believe, ultimately, is because "the Spirit of truth... whom I myself will send from the Father, will *bear witness* on my behalf." We know the Father because the Spirit is crying, "Abba! Father!" in our hearts. And it is only by the same Spirit that we can say and know that "Jesus is Lord."[2]

The Spirit bears witness to us that we know the Father and the Son by moving us to *act* on what we believe. Jesus said, "You must bear witness as well." We can't be sure our faith is real until we see its effects. Faith is like pregnancy: no one knows it is there until it shows.

Sometimes we recognize the Spirit in us by contrast. When others make fun of our ideals or think we are crazy because of what we give priority to, we need to ask, "Why do I see this if they don't?" Are we any smarter? Do we even necessarily feel we are better persons than they are? But we know we know. And if we know, how do we explain that, if not by the Spirit given to us?

When we realize that what we know and desire is God's free gift to us, then not only does *"the Lord takes delight in his people"*; we take delight in him.

[1] *John* 16:27
[2] *Romans* 8:15-16; *Galatians* 4:6; *1Corinthians* 12:3.

Decision: Acknowledge the Spirit. Tell God you believe, you hope, you love.

TUESDAY SIXTH WEEK OF EASTER

MAY 31, 2011

Feast of The Visitation of the Blessed Virgin Mary

The *Responsorial* (*Isaiah* 12:2-6) tells us the response that should be evoked from everyone who sees how Christians live: *"Among you is the great and Holy One of Israel."*

Romans 12:9-16 (alternate: *Zephaniah* 3:14-18) is like a description of *prophetic witness*. It lists ways of acting—and, more deeply, of *being*—that should be visible in every Christian's life. They are so different from the standards of any human culture, that only the presence of the risen Jesus, acting through his Spirit in those who believe, can explain them.

- To love everyone "with the affection of brothers and sisters." No strangers.
- To be proactive in showing respect for everyone. Repeat: everyone.
- To perform every task enthusiastically, as a way of "serving the Lord."
- When things are tough, to "rejoice" in a hope sustained by persevering prayer.
- To (choose to) feel about others' need the same way you feel about your own.
- To be generous in opening your home to others, your country to immigrants.
- To pray for the good of those who make your life hell instead of cursing them.
- To gravitate toward those who are unhappy as well as those fun to be with.
- To forget about social status and mix with those who can't help you.

St. Paul continues the list. Translate it into modern forms as food for thought.

In **Luke 1:39-56** we see the effect that the presence of God in us should have on others. All Mary did was show up on Elizabeth's doorstep. The effect on Elizabeth was not all miracle. True, "the baby stirred in her womb for joy." But something also stirred in Elizabeth's heart just from what she saw in Mary's face, or knew of her already, that her appearance recalled. What was that?

It was what Mary believed. What she knew from the word of God, and by the Holy Spirit: the truth, the values, the convictions she embraced and lived by. What she *was*. And what was that?

Her *Canticle* gives the core of it:

- She lived and breathed to "proclaim the goodness of the Lord." This was her "soul," her very being.
- She sought and found her *joy* in God. God was her "savior": the source, sustainer, and summit of all that could make her happy.
- She knew God *accepted* her, and intended to *use* her for "great things," although in herself she was nothing.
- She knew she was not the exception: "his mercy is from age to age" on *all* those who respect him for what he is.
- She recognized that God's values are not those of this world. The "proud" are "confused"; the "mighty" are insecure in their lofty positions; the "rich" who think they have "every good thing" are in fact "empty." The truly blessed are the humble, the lowly, and the poor. Her Son will proclaim this later in his "Beatitudes."[1]

When Christians live by these truths, all sincere people will cry out, *"Among you is the great and Holy One of Israel."*

[1] See *Matthew* 5:1-12 and the *Spiritual Exercises* of St. Ignatius of Loyola, nos. 136-147. Christ counters the strategy of the devil—desire for *riches* which bring *prestige* and lead to *pride*—by urging preference for a *poverty* that identifies one with the humiliated "*lowly*" and fosters *humility*.

Decision: Sing Mary's *Canticle*—not in words, but in lifestyle.

SAME DAY: MAY 31, 2011

The *Responsorial* (*Psalm* 138) cap-
sulizes the Good News: *"Your right
hand has saved me, O Lord."*

Acts 16:22-34 reveals again the pattern
of evangelization. First there is *pre-
evangelization*: an event that shocks,
that raises a question. Here it is not so
much the earthquake itself as the fact
that the prisoners did not leave. The
jailer, impressed by all this, asks the
question: "What must I do to be saved?"
That opens the door for the second
step: *evangelization*, or announcing the
Good News in response to a desire to
hear it. Paul and Silas said, "Believe in
the Lord Jesus and you will be saved,
you and all your household." The guard
brought them to his family and the disciples "proceeded to announce the
word of God to him and to everyone in
his house." In response "he and his
whole family were baptized." Then, in a
preview of *Eucharist*, step three, the
guard "spread a table before them and
joyfully celebrated with his whole family his newfound faith in God."

In the Mass, the *Introductory Rites* are
evangelization, but also pre-evangelization. The joy the community expresses in the entrance hymn; the
Greeting that presents the shocking
concepts: "the grace of the Lord Jesus
Christ, love of God, communion in the
Holy Spirit…"; the total acceptance of
all by all taken for granted in the *Penitential Rite* with the *"Lord, have mercy"*;
the phrases of the *Gloria*—all these
should raise questions in believers and
visitors alike. The *Liturgy of the Word*
begins to answer them. Then all are invited to *respond* by "coming forward,"
represented by the bread and wine in
the *Presentation of Gifts,* to express
their belief and their continuing but renewed acceptance of Baptism: placing
themselves on the altar to be offered
with and in Jesus during the *Eucharistic Prayer.* The *Rite of Communion* follows in anticipation of the "wedding
banquet of the Lamb." It is all the Good
News celebrated: *"Your right hand has
saved me, O Lord."*

In **John 16:5-11** Jesus says it is better
he should leave this earth and return
to live in and through us than to stay
here in the body he got from Mary. He
gives three reasons:

1. The lives of prophetic witness that
the Spirit empowers us to live, plus the
manifest "fruit of the Spirit" in us (see
Galatians 5:22), give proof worldwide
that Jesus gives what he promised. It
shows that refusal to believe in him is
"sin," a rejection of obvious good.

2. Jesus was unjustly condemned: we
"see him no more." But when we act in
ways inexplicable without his Spirit, it
proves God's *justice* triumphed. Jesus
visibly alive and acting everywhere in
us reveals that death simply returned
him to the Father. He is in glory. The
"gift of the Spirit" in us is proof of it.

3. The Spirit empowering us to live by
Christ's values over those of the culture
is proof of *judgment* against "the prince
of this world." God doesn't sit back and
let evil triumph. Jesus has "overcome
the world" (*John* 16:33; *1John* 4:4). We
proclaim it: *"Your right hand has saved
me, O Lord."*

Decision: Be Christ: Live by the Spirit to reveal him in the flesh.

JUNE 1, 2011

The *Responsorial* (*Psalm* 148) declares God is evident everywhere: *"Heaven and earth are filled with your glory."*

When we first gave ourselves to God in Baptism, we either knew nothing about God (if we were baptized as infants), or we knew less than we know now. Every day we learn a little more, both by discipleship and by experience, about who God is, what the mystery of Christian life is, and what it means to live it out in practice. That is why, each time at Mass when we re-present our "bodies to God as a living sacrifice" in the *Presentation of Gifts* by sending up a host that represents us to be placed on the altar and offered as Christ, we do it with more understanding of the commitment we are making. And more understanding of the God to whom we are making it. And more appreciation of the mystery involved in receiving and living the grace of Baptism.

In **Acts 17:15 to 18:l** Paul is urging this kind of growth to the people of Athens who, though sophisticated and intellectual, still had no clear concept of an infinite God. They worshiped many gods, symbolic personifications of many human truths and values. And there was value in their worship, insofar as it made them focus on certain real values of human life and dedicate themselves to realizing them. Vulcan, for example, was the personification of technology; Mercury of speed; Aphrodite of fertility; Venus of sexual love; Bacchus of celebration. Their devotion to these and many other "gods" revealed and fostered their apprecia-

tion for these values, all good, and all very respected elements in modern life and culture—as they should be. But for many of us, some of these values are just as much "idols" as they were for the Athenians. We just don't name them as our "gods."

Paul is not arguing against dedication to human values. He simply takes our thinking a step further by pointing out that recognition of these values, whether individually or collectively, falls far short of acknowledging "the God who made the world and everything in it, the Lord of heaven and earth," the infinite Creator and Giver of being. The mystery of this God, Paul says, is that "in him we live and move and have our being." This God embraces all created reality, including ourselves.

Have we grown into an understanding of the God Paul proclaims? God who is All Good, All we can desire on earth or in heaven? All we live for? For us, are *"heaven and earth filled with his glory"*?

In **John 16:12-15** Jesus says to his disciples, "I have much more to tell you, but you cannot bear it now. When the Spirit of truth comes, however, he will guide you to all truth."

Christianity is life, and life is progressive. We gradually grow into greater understanding of our faith, greater intentionality in our hope, greater absorption in our love for God and others. This again is a reason to recommit ourselves repeatedly in the *Presentation of Gifts*: it takes more than one lick to drive a nail home.

Decision: Keep recommitting as experience opens you to receive and give more.

June 2, 2011

These are today's readings where the feast of the Ascension has been transferred to the Seventh Sunday of Easter. Where not, see June 5 for the feast of the Ascension.

The *Responsorial* (*Psalm* 98) proclaims God's irrepressible "steadfast love": *"The Lord has revealed to the nations his saving power."*

In **Acts 18:1-8** Paul is not having much success in Corinth converting his fellow Jews, whether of Jewish or Greek origin. When they "turned against him and started to insult him," he finally said, "Your blood be on your own heads!... From now on I will go to the Gentiles." Nevertheless, "Crispus, president of the synagogue, and his whole household, all became believers… and a great many Corinthians who heard Paul… were baptized." God doesn't give up. Someone has called him "the God of second chances." And third, and fourth, until we have entered fully into death. This is really just another way of recognizing him as the God of "steadfast love," which is Scripture's most characteristic description of him.

In **John 16:16-20** Jesus says something to his apostles that has application to our daily experience: "A little while, and you will no longer see me, and again a little while, and you will see me."

All of us have the experience of being "turned on" by God, or by some religious activity, such as private prayer or the Mass, and later being "turned off" by exactly the same thing. What we call "devotion" and the spiritual writers call "consolation," just doesn't last. It comes and goes. Saint Ignatius gives reasons for this in his *Spiritual Exercises*,[1] but the essential is to know it is normal and expect it. And above all, to know that the "desolation," or lack of all feelings of devotion—sometimes extending to the absence of all feeling of conviction about the faith, of love, or even of any felt interest in God—will not last. "You will be sorrowful, but your sorrow will turn into joy." You will be "turned on" again, and when you are, you will know that it is by God, and not just because the liturgy is more exciting for a change, or you have begun to do something different in prayer. This is when we experience grace most purely as grace and Jesus most clearly as God.

A clarification, however: When we don't find devotion we should first examine what we ourselves are doing at Mass, in prayer or in action. We may need to make some changes. The first one at Mass is just to *pay attention to the words*. The words are exciting. But only if we think about what they mean.

The essential response, however, is just to reaffirm our faith, hope, and love: not "even when," but "especially when" we don't feel it. Faith, hope, and love are gifts from God, but each is also a free choice. The grace of each is the grace to *choose to act* by faith, in hope, with love. That is why the *Presentation of Gifts* is such a crucial moment in Mass: it is the explicit invitation to reaffirm our Baptism and all it expresses. If we persevere, we will say, *"the Lord has revealed… his saving power."*

[1] See no. 322

Decision: Go up in spirit with the bread and wine at Mass. Be placed on the altar.

JUNE 3, 2011

What the *Responsorial* (*Psalm* 47) says is not always obvious: *"God is king of all the earth."* But it is still true.

The truth is, we see God's will flaunted constantly—even by ourselves. The good he desires is not done. The evil he hates is inflicted on countless victims. We are tempted to ask, "Who is in charge?" It does not appear to be God.

In **Acts 18:9-18** the Lord tells Paul not to worry: "There are many of my people in this city." God supports free will, which by definition means he allows evil to happen. But he is still in charge, and there are people who listen to him.

In the Catholic Church there is a way we are failing to listen to God that we may not notice. It is the failure to call Church authorities to accountability. The laity are as guilty of this as anyone.

We are shocked to read that when the proconsul Gallio dismissed the Jews' case against Paul, "they all turned on Sosthenes, the synagogue president, and beat him in front of the court house." This was clearly bad. But whenever something goes wrong, we do tend to blame whoever is in charge. And with some justification. Authorities admit, "The buck stops here." They *are* responsible for the good of the community. If there are abuses, they should correct them. If they do not, they should be confronted as Paul confronted Peter for his cowardice as Pope![1] But Catholics, out of a false sense of reverence for priests and bishops, allow them repeatedly to deaden the Church by refusing to correct abuses and failing to lead the Church forward.

An underlying negligence surfaced in the child abuse scandal, which erupted in the United States, flowed out to Ireland and Germany, and is probably going to inundate the rest of the world before the lava cools. The abuse itself is not a specifically Catholic issue: most abusers are family members, and there are as many or more in state institutions as in the priesthood. But the bishops' complicity is a specifically Catholic sin, made possible in part by the laity's assumption that priests should not be turned over immediately to the police, or that their bishops were so holy they would make the proper moral response. No one would say that as soon as a bishop was known to have reassigned a child-abuser priest, the laity should have "all turned on him, and beat him in front of the [chancery office]." That would have been a sin. But surely a lesser sin than allowing the abuse to continue.

God draws good out of evil. In **John 16:20-23** Jesus could be saying to the Church today: "You will weep and mourn [and you should, for what you have failed to do] but the world will rejoice." Only a sin of the Catholic Church could draw such widespread, worldwide attention. If that attention serves to deter future child abusers and to encourage victims to report them to the police immediately, "the world will rejoice." Even more so if it wakes up Catholics to their duty to challenge all church officials about everything they are doing to, or not doing for, the flock.

[1] *Galatians* 2:11-14.

Decision: Accept responsibility. Do your part to keep the Church on course.

JUNE 4, 2011

In **Acts 18:23-28** we meet Apollos, a Jew who "knew only the baptism of John," but was "well-versed in the scriptures, instructed in the Way of the Lord, spoke with burning enthusiasm, and taught accurately the things concerning Jesus." When the Christian community heard him speak, they "took him aside and explained the Way of God to him more accurately," and encouraged him in his ministry.

Apollos reminds us of what Baptism commits us to do. We are not all eloquent speakers, but there is no excuse for any of us not to be "well-versed in the scriptures, instructed in the Way of the Lord," and filled with "burning enthusiasm" to spread the Good News. Whether or not it was ever impressed on us, we are all called to be evangelizers, because "the Church exists to evangelize," and we are the Church.[1]

To evangelize, we don't have to stand up and preach, or go door-to-door explaining our religion to strangers. But we do have to *desire* to spread the Good News. This does not mean telling people about Church doctrines—although, when asked, we should be able, like Apollos, to explain "accurately the things concerning Jesus." The most important thing is to share our *experience* of Jesus Christ, because that is our true experience of the Good News, and without that no discussions about doctrine are going to get anywhere. It is not what we know that reaches hearts, but what we are. If what we are has been transformed by our personal interaction with Jesus

Christ, we have good news to share. And will want to.

In **John 16:23-28** Jesus emphasizes the difference between religion that informs and religion that transforms. He tells his apostles, who had heard him preach for three years, "Until now you have not asked for anything in my name." They have prayed as "followers" of Jesus or as "disciples" ("students"). But they did not know the transformation of "becoming Christ" by dying and rising with him in Baptism to live henceforth as his risen body on earth. This is a mystery; the mystery of our lives that transforms everything we do.

Before receiving the divine life of God and the "gift of the Spirit" through Baptism and Confirmation, we only knew *about* the Father. But now, with the Spirit of Jesus the Son crying out "Abba! Father!" in our hearts, Christ "tells us plainly of the Father." His Father and ours.[2]

At every Mass, during the *Presentation of Gifts*, the liturgy invites us to recommit consciously to Christ and to the life of grace. This makes us more aware of the difference between just being baptized and accepting Baptism with increasing understanding as we mature in both human and divine life. Experience teaches us what it means to "be Christ." As we enter more deeply and consciously into that experience, we become able to share the Good News.

[1]Paul VI, *Evangelization in the Modern World,* 14.
[2]*Romans* 8:16; *Galatians* 4:6.

Decision: Identify your experience of Christ. As you see it, share it.

FOR REFLECTION AND DISCUSSION: EASTER WEEK SIX

The Sixth Week of Easter: The crown of conversion is the *gift of the Holy Spirit*. When our lifestyle raises questions, we should be able to answer out of our *experience* of the Spirit giving inner joy and power. Especially in *choices* we make that no merely human knowledge or experience would justify. Especially love.

Invitation: Seek conscious, experienced *joy in the Spirit* as a constitutive element of true Christian life. Joy is found in loving.

Ask yourself in prayer and others in discussion: How could the statements below make Mass mean more if we stay aware of them during Mass?

Acts 16:11-15: We *express* our faith and love in the *Presentation of Gifts* so we ourselves will be convinced that we believe—personally, consciously, freely.

John 15:26 to 16:4: The way we know we believe, ultimately, is because the Spirit bears witness within us by moving us to *act* on what we believe.

Acts 16:22-34: The Mass follows the pattern of evangelization: the *Introductory Rites* raise a *question* that the *Liturgy of the Word* begins to *answer*. Then in the *Presentation of Gifts,* all *respond* by symbolically "coming forward."

Acts 17:15 to 18:1: For many, some human values are just as much "idols" as they were for the Athenians. We just don't name them as our "gods."

Christianity is life, and life is progressive. We grow gradually. This is a reason to recommit ourselves repeatedly in the *Presentation of Gifts.*

Acts 18:1-8: God is "the God of second chances" and "steadfast love." We express this in the *Presentation of Gifts* by repeated recommitment.

John 16:16-20: It is normal that "consolation" and "desolation" do not last. The essential response to this is just to reaffirm our faith, hope, and love, especially when we don't feel anything. That is why the *Presentation of Gifts* is such a crucial moment in Mass: it is an explicit invitation to reaffirm our Baptismal commitment.

Acts 18:9-18: Catholics, out of a false sense of reverence for priests and bishops, allow them repeatedly to deaden the Church by refusing to correct abuses and failing to lead the Church forward. We have a duty to challenge church officials.

Acts 18:23-28: There is no excuse for any of us not to be "well-versed in the Scriptures," instructed, and burning with enthusiasm to spread the Good News.

John 16:23-28: The *Presentation of Gifts* emphasizes the difference between religion that informs and religion that transforms. We re-commit to *mystery*.

Decisions:

Let the Spirit move you to find your joy in loving consciously in everything you do.
Be Christ: Live by the Spirit to reveal him in the flesh.
Keep recommitting as experience opens you to receive and give more.
Go up in spirit with the bread and wine at Mass. Be placed on the altar.
Accept responsibility. Do your part to keep the Church on course.

SUNDAY, JUNE 5 2011

Except in the provinces of Boston, Hartford, New York, Newark, Philadelphia, and Omaha the Feast of the Ascension is transferred from the sixth Thursday of Easter to the seventh Sunday of Easter. Where it is not transferred, see the next reflection.

INVENTORY

What does it mean to me that Jesus ascended into heaven? Does it have any influence on my life? On the decisions I make today?

INPUT

The *Entrance Antiphon* tells us to stop "looking up at the skies" because, just as Jesus left, in the same way he is going to return. The *Opening Prayer* has us ask that we might "follow him into the new creation," and calls his ascension "our joy, our glory, and our hope." The *Responsorial* (*Psalm* 47) just calls for celebration: "*God mounts his throne to shouts of joy; a blare of trumpets for the Lord.*"

This is a lot to deal with! Taken together, these texts call us to "await the blessed hope and the coming of our Savior, Jesus Christ" (from the *Communion Rite* of the Mass). But this is an *active* waiting: we don't just stand around waiting for it to happen; we are *sent* to *make* it happen.

THE REIGN OF GOD

Acts 1:1-11 tells us that after his resurrection, Jesus spent forty days appearing to his apostles and "speaking about the reign of God." We don't know what he said, but the apostles must not have understood, because just before Jesus ascended they still thought he was going to set up a government in Israel supported by divine power! "Lord is this the time when you will restore the kingdom to Israel?"

Jesus didn't answer; he just kept telling them to "wait"—wait for the "fulfillment of my Father's promise," wait to be "baptized with the Holy Spirit," wait to "receive power when the Holy Spirit comes down on you." Then "*You will be my witnesses* in Jerusalem, in all Judea and Samaria, and to the ends of the earth." The kingdom is going to be established by divine power, but working through human weakness. It will be the power of the Holy Spirit enlightening and motivating them; a Spirit not of coercion and force, but of conversion through truth and love.

This should have told them already that the establishment of God's reign over every human heart was going to take a long time! When we pray, "Thy kingdom come!" we are praying "Thy *will be done* on earth as in heaven." God's reign will not be complete until everyone really wants this.

AT GOD'S RIGHT HAND

Ephesians 1:17-23 tells us that in God's time-frame Jesus is already

SUNDAY Feast of The Ascension

reigning. God has "seated him at his right hand in the heavenly places, far above all rule and authority and power and dominion… not only in this age but also in the age to come. And he has put all things under his feet and has made him the head over all things for the Church, which is his body, the fullness of him who fills all in all." This is what the Ascension says: in Jesus *God mounts his throne to shouts of joy.* The man the apostles ate and drank and walked the dusty roads with, the man they saw crucified in weakness, is now seated at God's right hand in glory, and all power is his *now*—and forever. St. Paul writes this so that the "eyes of your heart may be enlightened," and "you may know what is the hope to which he has called you… and what is the immeasurable greatness of his power for us who believe." *"God mounts his throne to shouts of joy."* Our joy is the joy of our *hope.*

"Go Therefore…"

We need hope, unshakeable hope, because in **Matthew 28:16-20** Jesus tells the apostles and us: "Go *make disciples of all nations*, baptizing them… teaching them to obey everything I have commanded you."

That is hardly a modest undertaking! But Jesus empowers us with the words, "All authority in heaven and on earth has been given to me…. And remember, I am *with you always*, to the end of the world." Jesus ascended, not to leave us, but to remain with us, in every member of his body on earth who is animated by his Spirit. With us, in us, and through us, Jesus continues to "go about all the cities and villages, *teaching* … and *proclaiming* the good news of the kingdom, and *curing* every disease and every sickness" (*Matthew* 4:23; 9:35). This is his ministry. He will continue it in his body, the Church, until the reign of God is established in every heart that accepts him. Then he will "come again," his triumph revealed in the emergent glory of his body, his glory shining in diversified beauty through each and every member of the human race who has become a transparent vessel of God's own life and love.

Jesus ascends to make this happen. He ascends to send down the Holy Spirit. The Church professes her faith and hope in prayer: "Send forth your Spirit, and our *hearts will be regenerated.*" The Church believes this can happen. And then, *"You will renew the face of the earth!"* That is what we celebrate: *"God mounts his throne to shouts of joy; a blare of trumpets for the Lord."*

Insight
Does the Ascension of Jesus inspire you now to let him live and continue his work in you? Does his promise of the Holy Spirit encourage you? Does it motivate you to any decisions?

Initiative
Resolve to let Christ grow "to full stature" in you (Ephesians 4:13), and dedicate yourself to a lifestyle that bears witness, so that you can help bring Christ to "full stature" throughout the human race.

Same Sunday, June 5 2011

(For the provinces of Boston, Hartford, New York, Newark, Philadelphia, and Omaha)

Spirit and Flesh

Inventory

In the *Entrance Antiphon*, not only do we say that our heart prompts us to "seek your face," but we declare positively to God: "I seek it. Lord, do not hide from me." Am I making both of these statements personally or just repeating them because they are "in the book"? How do I "seek God's face"? Where? How?

Input

In the *Opening Prayer* we affirm both that Christ "lives with God in glory," and "promised to remain with us until the end of time." Both statements are verified when we see Christ "glorified" visibly on earth. Then the words of the *Gloria* at Mass: "We praise you for your glory," take on the ring of personal experience.

When we sing in the *Responsorial* (*Psalm* 27): "I believe that I shall see the goodness of the Lord in the land of the living," we mean we will see God's glory here on earth—in the "community of the living"—as well as in heaven.

History and Spirit

Acts 1:12-14 makes a point of listing again the names of the original Twelve Jesus chose to be the foundation of his Church (minus Judas). This is because they were unique witnesses to Jesus.

There had to be twelve of them to show that the Church was the continuation of the twelve tribes of Israel. John reports:

> And in the spirit [the angel]... showed me the holy city Jerusalem coming down out of heaven from God.... It has a great, high wall with twelve gates... and on the gates are inscribed the names of the twelve tribes of the Israelites.... And the wall of the city has twelve foundations, and on them are the twelve names of the twelve apostles of the Lamb (*Revelation* 21:9-12).

The Twelve also had to be historical witnesses. The replacement had to be "one of the men who have accompanied us during all the time that the Lord Jesus went in and out among us, beginning from the baptism of John until the day when he was taken up from us" (*Acts* 1:21-22). Still today, to be a fully authentic witness to Jesus, one has to be in historical continuity with the community of those who knew him during his earthly life.

Saint Paul would not have qualified as one of the Twelve, because he did not know Jesus before his resurrection. That is why Paul, although he had already been baptized and had been preaching for three years, went up to Jerusalem to "visit Cephas [Peter] and stayed with him fifteen days." Then after fourteen years, "in response to a revelation" he went up again to Jerusalem with Barnabas and Titus, his co-workers, for "a private meeting with the acknowledged leaders." There, he says, "I laid before them the gospel that I proclaim among the Gentiles, in order to make sure that I was not running, or had not run, in vain." And he was approved. "When James and Cephas and John, who were acknowledged pillars, recognized the grace that had been given to me, they gave to Barnabas and me the right hand of fellowship, agreeing that we should go to the Gentiles and they to the circumcised" (*Galatians* 1:18; 2:1-9).

The Church Paul helped to establish is "built upon the foundation of the apostles and prophets, with Christ Jesus himself as the cornerstone" (*Ephesians* 2:20). The apostles are the link with the historical Jesus. But the prophets are proof that the risen Jesus is alive and speaking in the Church today through his Spirit. Both are essential. Jesus told the disciples before his Ascension, "not to leave Jerusalem, but to wait there for the promise of the Father.... *You will receive power* when the Holy Spirit has come upon you" (*Acts* 1:4-8). And that is why today's reading, after listing the apostles' names, shows them gathered in an upstairs room, "constantly devoting themselves to prayer."

CHRIST IN YOU, THE HOPE OF GLORY

John 17:1-11 says Jesus is "glorified" in us. This means that his "glory," his greatness and his triumph as Messiah and Savior of the world is made evident in us. We are the visible proof that he is what he claimed to be.

Jesus said to the Father, "I glorified you on earth by finishing *the work that you gave me to do."* We glorify Jesus by doing the work he gave us to do. And that work is made specific for us in our baptismal consecration: we were anointed at Baptism to fulfill the triple mission of Jesus as *Prophet, Priest,* and *King.* We glorify him because when we do his work, it becomes evident that Jesus is risen, alive, and doing the work himself—*with* us, *in* us, and *through* us.

Jesus was specific about the work the Father gave him. It was "to give eternal life" to all whom the Father gave him. Our work on earth is to be the instruments through which Jesus continues to "give eternal life"—that is, to communicate to others "the grace of our Lord Jesus Christ," which is the gift of sharing in the divine life of God.

"This is eternal life," Jesus said: "that they may *know you*, the only true God, and Jesus Christ whom you have sent." This was his work: "I have *made your name known* to those whom you gave me." Jesus lived and breathed to bring about the first thing he taught us to pray for: *"Father, hallowed be thy name!"* This was the first priority of his life, the greatest desire of his heart.

Jesus made the Father known by *embodying* in himself the truth and goodness of the Father. "Whoever sees me sees him who sent me" (*John* 12:45). When Philip said, "Lord, show us the Father, and we will be satisfied," he answered, "Have I been with you all this time, Philip, and you still do not know me? Whoever has seen me has seen the Father" (*John* 14:8-9). For us to glorify Jesus, people have to see him in us, alive and revealing himself in "works"—the choices that characterize our lifestyle—that are manifestly impossible by human motivation alone, but only by the power of his Spirit acting in us. This is to be *prophets.*

Jesus glorified the Father by being the visible "image of the invisible God" (*Colossians* 1:15) and "reflection of God's glory" (*Hebrews* 1:3). He continues to glorify the Father in his body, the Church. The life, the truth, the goodness, and glory of God are made visible now in those in whom the risen Jesus continues to *express himself* visibly on earth. Jesus said of his disciples, "I am no longer in the world, but they are in the world." He is "glorified in them" when we *communicate* his truth through the expression of our faith, his intentions through the expression of our hope, his love through the attitude we express toward all whom we deal with.

Of himself Jesus said, "Believe me that I am *in the Father* and the Father is in me; but if you do not, then believe me because of the works themselves." "The Father who *dwells in me* does his works." Of his disciples Jesus said, "The one who believes in me will also do the works that I do and, in fact, will do greater works than these." Jesus will work in and through them. We glorify the Son by making his life visible in us by *expressing* our faith, hope, and love.

St. Ireneus said, "Life in humans is the glory of God; the life of humans is the vision of God"—provided what is seen cannot be explained except by the "grace of our Lord Jesus Christ" risen and living his divine life *in us.*

Jesus said, "In a little while the world will no longer see me, but... because I live, you also will live…. On that day you will know that I am *in my Father,* and *you in me, and I in you*" (see *John* 14:10-20). Paul preached "the riches of the glory of this mystery, which is *Christ in you,* the hope of glory" (*Colossians* 1:26-27). To let Jesus in us *express himself* in and through our human expressions of faith, hope, and love is our ministry as *priests.*

THE GLORY OF "ENDURING LOVE"

1Peter 4:13-16 encourages us to "rejoice insofar as you are sharing Christ's sufferings, so that you may also be glad and shout for joy when his *glory* is revealed." The fact is, his glory is already revealed—here and now—in those who "are reviled for the name of Christ," because "the spirit of glory, which is the Spirit of God" is made visible in our "enduring love"—provided, of course, it is our hope in that "glory" which strengthens our love to endure. Then we suffer, not as "criminals or mischief makers," but as *"stewards of the kingship of Christ,"* striving and suffering for the establishment of his Kingdom.

"If any of you suffers as a Christian, do not consider it a disgrace, but glorify God because you bear this name" and are letting him reveal his empowering Spirit in you.

INSIGHT
Can I draw courage from knowing Jesus is "seated at the right hand of God"?

INITIATIVE
When you take a prophetic stance, imagine Jesus in power and glory.

JUNE 6, 2011

The *Responsorial* (*Psalm* 68) invites us to celebrate what we know of God: *"Sing to God, O kingdoms of the earth."*

Acts 19:1-8 makes clear that God does not just want to give us divine life. He wants us to know we have received it. And he wants others to see it in us. This is the reason for the "gift of the Spirit."

We would say today that those baptized by John the Baptizer received "the grace of the Lord Jesus Christ," even though the true nature of this gift was not yet revealed and they had no idea what they had received. Paul asked them, "Did you receive the Holy Spirit when you became believers?" If he had asked instead, "Did you receive divine life when you were baptized?" their answer would have been the same: "We never even heard of it." Unfortunately, many of the baptized today would say the same thing. How many are deeply, consciously aware of sharing in the divine life of God himself? It should make us want to genuflect to ourselves!

We may have learned this during our religious instruction—but as an abstract truth that didn't sink in and didn't really mystify or astound us. We probably didn't connect it to our life or experience. The "gift of the Spirit" does.

We are aware of having received the "gift of the Spirit" when we experience things in ourselves—feelings, perhaps, but more reliably *convictions, attitudes, values,* and *actions* empowered by these—that have no human explanation; that can only be the fruit of God's divine life within us. We may not "begin to speak with tongues and to prophesy" as Paul's Christians did. But we will feel impelled to cry out in some way: *"Sing to God, O kingdoms of the earth."* We know that we have *become divine.* And we rejoice.

In **John 16:29-33** Christ's own disciples did not fully understand who he was. But when he answered a question they hadn't asked, they said, "Now we see that you know everything, and do not have to wait for questions to be put into words. Because of this we believe that you came from God." They still did not understand he was God, but at least they knew that nothing human could explain him. To speak and act in ways that let people see the same truth in us is the essence of Christian *witness.* We are consecrated to this by our baptismal anointing as *prophets.* When we do bear witness in this way, the "gift of the Spirit" becomes visible in us.

Our sharing in divine life is the key to Baptism. This is made explicit in the *Presentation of Gifts.* The presider prays as he pours a little water into the wine before presenting it to God:

> By the mystery of [the mingling of] this water and wine, *may we come to share in the divinity of Christ,* who humbled himself to share in our humanity.

The wine represents divinity, the water humanity. We mingle them to remind us of the "mystery" of the human and divine united in Jesus by his Incarnation, and in us by our Baptism.

This reminder of what we are reminds us of what we should do. We need to let our divine life appear in actions that reveal the "gift of the Spirit" who empowers us to live on the level of God.

Decision: Pay attention during the *Presentation of Gifts.* Absorb the meaning.

JUNE 7, 2011

Today's verses of the *Responsorial* (*Psalm 68*) invite us to *"Sing to God"* for his *generosity* in pouring out divine life like rain.

In **Acts 20:17-27** Paul describes how God's divine life was made visible in him. Not through miracles, visions, or ecstasies (although all these are found in his life). He just says, "I carried out the *mission* the Lord Jesus gave me." It was "to bear *witness* to the Good News of God's grace." How did he do this?

> I lived among you… serving the Lord with all humility… enduring the trials that came to me… I have not hesitated to do anything that would be helpful to you. I have preached to you, and instructed you both in public and in your homes, urging both Jews and Greeks to turn to God and to believe in our Lord Jesus.

None of this strikes us as being so explicitly "divine"—until we ask ourselves how many people we see doing the same, and for what motives.

Plenty of non-Christians and even atheists are dedicated to serving people, and are willing to "do anything helpful" for others if they can, "enduring the trials" that come to them as a result. Do their lives reveal God's life in them?

Let's not rule it out. They may well be what we call "anonymous Christians," people who have surrendered to the grace of God, but under some other name because for them "the true nature of God and of religion" was "concealed rather than revealed" by the Church they experienced. Vatican II lays blame on Catholics, lay and clergy alike, who "are careless about their instruction in the faith, or present its teaching falsely, or even fail in their religious, moral, or social life." We have taught errors.[1]

The key question, though, is motive. Some people "do good" (and it is good), just because it is humanly rewarding. Also, their social milieu may support feeling disturbed by the disorder and irrationality of injustice, ecological devastation, sickness, and suffering. They feel better trying to set things right. Add human compassion and we have love. Some have argued that all love reveals divine grace, but this leads to the conclusion that humans cannot love without grace, which makes human nature radically corrupt. So we must say it is possible to be loving and altruistic without grace. But we never can or should judge this is actually so in a particular case.

For Christian witness, however, it needs to be obvious that human motives cannot explain what one does. And this can appear in very ordinary ministries such as Paul details, especially if they are constant and enduring enough to reveal persevering commitment.

In **John 17:1-11** Jesus saw his crucifixion as the supreme and unambiguous revelation of his divine love, both for God and humans. "Father, the hour has come. Glorify your Son so that the Son may glorify you." He in turn is glorified in those disciples whose lives make it clear they "know the Father and Jesus whom he sent." This, Jesus says, "is eternal life." Our persevering love shows that we know God.

[1] See *Vatican II*, "The Church in the Modern World," no. 19, and "The Church," no. 51.

Decision: Recommit to revealing the light in you that is proof of eternal life.

JUNE 8, 2011

Both readings express the concern Jesus and Paul have for the protection of the flock after they are gone. So today's invitation to *"Sing to God"* (*Responsorial, Psalm* 68) focuses on God's power to "strengthen his people."

In **Acts 20:28-38** Paul warns the "elders" (priests) and "overseers" (bishops): "Some even from your own group will come distorting the truth." The Vatican Council accepts this as the normal condition of the "pilgrim Church" and so "urges all concerned to remove or correct any abuses, excesses, or defects which may have crept in here or there," even in the official teaching of the "ordinary *magisterium*" of bishops, preachers, and teachers. The Church does not claim to be perfect in any age.[1]

That is why we always have need of the "prophets;" those who, like Paul, "bear witness… to the primacy of an inward communion of faith and love, the perpetually new work of the Spirit." This, of course, must be in union with the "primacy of Peter," which it complements: the primacy of juridical authority in the Church, given to Peter with the "keys of the kingdom."[2]

And "therein hangs the tale" of ever-recurring conflict in the Church: true prophets against false prophets, the *magisterium* squelching truth, teachers of error ignoring the *magisterium*. Jesus and Paul both predicted it would happen. How do we survive?

We survive, first of all, by absolute, unconditional *commitment* to remain united to the Church that celebrates *Eucharist* in union with all the bishops throughout the world who trace their commission back to the Twelve. This is a non-negotiable. We may argue about all sorts of things, but we must never actually break with the bishops.

We express this in every Mass. The *Liturgy of the Word* may invite different interpretations, and we may disagree strongly with the homilist, but our next move is to join ourselves to the bread and wine being placed on the altar and present ourselves unconditionally to be offered with Christ in the Church. Doing this consciously and intensely in every Mass will keep us from losing the faith.

In **John 17:11-19** Jesus asks the Father, "Keep those you have given me true to your name, so they may be one like us." He bases his prayer on the statement: "They do not belong to the world, any more than I belong to the world." Those who have given up attachment to all the world offers—especially to riches, power and prestige—will have the least to divide them from one another. Regardless of differences of opinion on current questions of doctrine and pastoral practice, if they share with each other their prayer, their devotion, and their experience of God, the "grace of the Lord Jesus Christ" will fill them with "the love of God" and each other, and they will find "communion in the Holy Spirit." They will be able to lead us in proclaiming: *"Sing to God, O kingdoms of the earth."*

[1]Vatican II: *The Church*, no. 51.
[2]See J. M. R. Tillard, O.P., *The Bishop of Rome*, Glazier, Inc., 1986, pages 74-117.

Affirm: In commitment to truth, unity; in pursuit of truth, liberty; in all, charity.

JUNE 9, 2011

The *Responsorial* (*Psalm* 16) provides deep support for loyalty: *"Keep me safe, O God; you are my hope."*

In **Acts 22:30 to 23:11** we see Paul uniting in himself fidelity to the charismatic and to the juridical. He follows the voice of the Spirit, but insists on his obedience to the Law.

We may be shocked to hear Paul claiming, "Brothers, I am a Pharisee." We need to remember that the Pharisees began as an authentically Jewish reform movement based on fidelity to the Law. This was what God called for constantly through the prophets. It became corrupted only gradually, as it degenerated into narrow legalism. A focus on law observance that does not pass through contemplation of the mind and heart of God is deadly. But law observance as such is good. It is fidelity to God, and Paul claimed it for himself. He also claimed fidelity to the Spirit who can never be restricted to laws. In this he embodied Christianity.

Christianity is essentially the union of the human and the divine. Laws belong to the human side. Laws are the infinite, indivisible, and ultimately undifferentiated Wisdom and Love of God translated into finite human concepts; broken down into particular directions to guide concrete human actions. Laws are by nature "defined" by *fines*, limits, specifications. We must keep in mind that they are always imperfect translations of the Infinite, and we must observe them in conscious submission to the Infinite Truth and Goodness they can never completely express. We *ob-serve* laws, but we only *serve* the Spirit.

The prayer that accompanies the mingling of water (for humanity) and wine (for divinity) during the *Presentation of Gifts* captures this:

> By the mystery of [the mingling of] this water and wine, *may we come to share in the divinity of Christ*, who humbled himself to *share in our humanity.*

Jesus, who was above the Law, subjected himself to the Law, but without contradiction, because he was the Law made flesh. When we who have "become Christ" by Baptism follow the Spirit, it is the spirit of the law we follow. This is not to "abolish the law but to fulfill it. This is our mission as *prophets.* Only God can keep us authentic. *"Keep me safe, O God; you are my hope."*[1]

Once mixed, the water and wine are indistinguishable, as were humanity and divinity in the actions of Jesus. In **John 17:20-26** Jesus prays that, in spite of the incompleteness of every human insight, opinion, or perception of value; in spite of the incompleteness of all human expressions of doctrine and the unintentional exclusivity of all human laws—that cannot explicitly adapt themselves to every exception or particular application—his Church will be one: "Father, may they be one *in us*, as you are in me and I am in you." The human inevitably tends to divide us. The divine unites us. *In Christ* both are one.

[1]*John* 14:6; *Matthew* 5:17.

Decision: Follow the Spirit in a spiritual observance of all laws.

JUNE 10, 2011

The *Responsorial* (*Psalm* 103) calls us to look to God alone in our decisions: *"The Lord has set his throne in heaven."*

Acts 25:13-21 brings to a head a whole series of people refusing to accept the responsibility of decision. The tribune, although he found Paul "was charged with nothing deserving death or imprisonment," passed him on to the governor Felix to be judged. Felix put off making a decision for two years, until he was succeeded in office by Festus. Festus heard the charges, knew they were groundless, but "wishing to do a favor for the Jews," did not make a decision either. Instead he asked Paul, "Do you wish to go up to Jerusalem," as his enemies had requested, "and be tried there before me on these charges?" Paul, who saw which way the wind was blowing with Festus, said, "If there is nothing to their charges against me, no one can turn me over to them. I appeal to the emperor." Now Festus got to pass the buck, and he sent Paul to Rome.

Actually, God wanted this so that Paul and Peter would die in the same place, giving united witness to the faith. But in itself, the whole story is a travesty of justice, brought about by people who, one after another, refused to take responsibility for making a decision.[1]

This is a refusal the *Presentation of Gifts* meets head on in the Mass. When the bread and wine are sent forward to be placed on the altar, every Christian present is confronted with a decision to make. It is the radical, adult, all-embracing decision to take one's life, one's

existence, into one's own hands and decide what to do with it. What we want to make of it. On whom we wish to bestow it. The invitation is to give ourselves, body and soul, to God, as we did on the day of our Baptism. But to give more consciously, with more understanding of what the gift of self entails—and gives us in return. The *Presentation of Gifts* is a crucial and a precious moment that urges us to break the inertia of indecision and indifference and embrace radical self-determination in a deep choice of "life to the full."

The peak of self-determination is self-surrender. Jesus said, "Those who lose their life for my sake will find it." That is what Baptism is: giving up life in this world in order to live divinely as the body of Christ. There is no greater love; there is no greater life.[2]

In **John 21:15-19** Jesus tells Peter, as he told Paul, about the surrender which will bring him into total life. And death:

> When you grow old, you will stretch out your hands and someone else will fasten a belt around you and take you where you do not wish to go. (He said this to indicate the kind of death by which he would glorify God.)

Then he gave Peter the "Great Commandment" that rules all pastoral ministry: "If you love me, *feed my sheep.*" Those who don't "pass the buck" will have the courage to make whatever decisions this calls for.

[1] *Acts* 23:11. See again J. M. R. Tillard, O.P., *The Bishop of Rome*, Glazier, Inc., 1986, pages 74-117.
[2] *Matthew* 16:25.

Decision: Embrace life. Use your freedom to give it away.

JUNE 11, 2011

Feast of Saint Barnabas, Apostle

The *Responsorial* (*Psalm* 98) celebrates the action of the Spirit in the Church: *"The Lord has revealed to the nations his saving power."*

Acts 11:21-26 and 13:1-3: Some Christians who fled the persecution in Jerusalem "spoke the word" in Antioch and "a great number became believers and were converted to the Lord." When the community in Jerusalem heard this, they sent Barnabas to Antioch. Barnabas went to Tarsus and recruited Paul (still called Saul) to help him. After about a year the community sent them both to Jerusalem with famine relief and they recruited John Mark, Barnabas' cousin, to work with them. Then, back in Antioch, while the community was "engaged in the liturgy of the Lord... the Holy Spirit spoke to them: 'Set apart Barnabas and Saul for me to do the work for which I have called them.'" Mark went too, but "deserted" them in Pamphylia and returned to Jerusalem. For this Paul refused to take him on their next mission. Barnabas argued with him, and

> the disagreement became so sharp that they parted company; Barnabas took Mark with him and sailed away to Cyprus. But Paul chose Silas and set out... through Syria....[1]

Paul reconciled with Mark, because he asked Timothy to send him during his captivity in Rome and found him a "useful helper in my ministry."

What we see here is, first, the community's involvement in sending people off on mission; second, the way they came to decisions: through prayer, fasting, and spiritual discernment, trying to recognize the inspirations of the Holy Spirit. And lastly, we see that even the saints had their faults and weaknesses. Paul thought Mark, who probably wrote the Gospel, had failed them; and he and Barnabas split up over it: two saints who could not work together! There is encouragement in that.

We still tend to assume that those who are saints must not have faults and weaknesses. We even extend this, no matter how illogical it is, to priests and bishops. Then when the clergy, whom we have put on a pedestal that never should have existed, fall into public sin, we are disillusioned! Even the ordinary, petty faults of priests or bishops who are stupid, arrogant, or unfeeling make us think less of "the Church." We judge the whole Church by the clergy, who make up far less than a tenth of one percent of her members! We forget that the Church does not select people to be priests or even bishops because they are considered outstanding Catholics. Bishops ordain those they think God is calling, and the pope appoints as bishops those he thinks he can trust to carry out his policies. If we want to know whom the Church considers representative Christians, we should look at those she canonizes, not at those she ordains. And even the saints had serious flaws! But through their weakness and ours, *"The Lord has revealed to the nations his saving power."* That is what we focus on.

[1] See *Acts* 13:5, 13; 15:36-41; *Colossians* 4:10; *2 Timothy* 4:9-11.

Decision: Don't assume that position gives holiness or holiness means perfection.

SATURDAY SEVENTH WEEK OF EASTER

SAME DAY: JUNE 11, 2011

Today's liturgy gives the end of both the *Acts of the Apostles* and John's Gospel. *Acts* ends focused on the coming death of Paul; *John* ends focused on the future death of Peter. The *Responsorial (Psalm* 11) says of both: *"The just will gaze on your face, O Lord."*

In **Acts 28:16-31** Paul, who has been sent as a prisoner to Rome, is portrayed as being pretty much in charge of the situation. First (chapter 26) he convinces King Agrippa of his innocence and tries to convert him! Then he predicts the loss of the ship they put him on for Rome. When they don't take his advice and the ship is about to be lost, he assures them there will be no loss of life. And there isn't. They run aground, as Paul said they would. Paul is bitten by a poisonous snake and is taken for a god because he remains unharmed. He heals the father of their host and many others, who load their ship with provisions when they sail. When they reach Rome, *Acts* says, "Paul spent the whole of the two years in his own rented lodging, welcoming all who came to visit him, proclaiming the kingdom of God and teaching the truth about the Lord Jesus Christ with complete freedom and without hindrance from anyone." Thus ends Paul's story in the *Acts of the Apostles.*

We know that eventually he was martyred in Rome. The same prophecy was made of both Peter and Paul. To Peter Jesus said, "You will stretch out your hands and someone else will fasten a belt around you and take you where you do not wish to go."

For Paul, the prophet Agabus "took Paul's belt, bound his own feet and hands with it, and said…'This is the way the Jews in Jerusalem will bind the man who owns this belt and will hand him over to the Gentiles.'" And so it was. But even bound, both were in control. They were supremely free to dispose of their lives as they chose.

Karl Rahner wrote, "The greatest free moment of life is death." By freely, willingly saying "Yes" to death we can take control of our whole existence and bestow it on God. Without reserves. Nothing left out. Irrevocably. Forever. There is no greater freedom, no greater control than this. Jesus, at the most exalted moment of his humiliation modeled it: "Father, into your hands I commend my spirit!" He had said:

> I lay down my life in order to take it up again. No one takes it from me, but I lay it down of my own accord. I have power to lay it down, and… take it up again. I have received this command from my Father.[1]

In the *Presentation of Gifts*, we say this with Christ. We reaffirm the death we accepted by anticipation in Baptism and the risen life it gave. No one can "take our life" from us if we have already chosen to bestow it on God.

John 21:20-25 ends: "There are many other things that Jesus did; if every one of them were written down… the world itself could not contain the books that would be written." Our lives are writing them now.

[1]*John* 10:17-18.

Decision: Put yourself on the altar at every Mass. Own your life by offering it.

78

FOR REFLECTION AND DISCUSSION:
EASTER WEEK SEVEN

The Seventh Week of Easter: The Twelve were witnesses to the historical Jesus. To be fully authentic witnesses to Jesus today, we must be in historical continuity with them through the bishops. But we need to be "prophets" as proof that Jesus is risen and speaking in the Church today. Both are essential.

Invitation: To glorify Jesus by continuing his triple mission as *Prophet, Priest,* and *King* according to our "messianic anointing" at Baptism. People see Jesus alive in us when we do what can only be done by the power of his Spirit acting in us. When "reviled for the name of Christ" we make the Spirit visible by our "enduring love."

Ask yourself in prayer and others in discussion: How could the statements below make Mass mean more if we stay aware of them during Mass?

Acts 19:1-8: We experience the "gift of the Spirit" in choices that can only be the fruit of God's divine life within us. God wants us to *know* and others to see this gift in us. In the *Presentation of Gifts* the Church wants us to present ourselves with the bread and wine so we will know and others see that we accept our Baptism.

John 16:29-33: In the *Presentation of Gifts* the wine represents divinity, the water humanity. We mingle them to remind us of the "mystery" of the human and divine united in Jesus by his Incarnation, and in us by our Baptism.

Acts 20:17-27: When human motives cannot explain what one does, this is Christian witness. This can appear in very ordinary actions if they are constant and enduring. **John 17:1-11** says that persevering love is what shows we know God.

Acts 20:28-38: Conflict between *prophets* (true and false) and the *magisterium* is normal in the "pilgrim Church" that does not claim to be perfect in any age. We survive by unconditional commitment to the Church. We express this by presenting ourselves without reserves to be placed on the altar with the bread and wine.

Acts 22:30 to 23:11: Christianity is essentially the union of the human and the divine. The prayer that accompanies the *Presentation of Gifts* affirms this: "By the mystery [of this mingling]… may we come to share…."

Laws are always imperfect human translations of the divine Truth and Goodness they can never completely express. We *ob-serve* laws, but we only *serve* the Spirit.

Acts 25:13-21: Paul's trial is a travesty of justice, brought about by people who refused to take the responsibility of decision. The *Presentation of Gifts* meets this problem by inviting everyone present to make the all-embracing decision to take their life into their hands and place it on the altar to be offered with and in Christ.

Acts 28:16-31: "The greatest free moment of life is death." In the *Presentation of Gifts* we reaffirm the death we freely accepted by anticipation in Baptism.

Decisions:

When you take a prophetic stance, imagine Jesus in power and glory.
Put yourself on the altar at every Mass. Own your life by offering it.
Pay attention during the *Presentation of Gifts.* Absorb the meaning.
Recommit to revealing the light in you that is proof of eternal life.
Affirm: In commitment to truth, unity; in pursuit of truth, liberty; in all, charity.
Follow the Spirit in a spiritual observance of all laws.
Embrace life. Use your freedom to give it away.

JUNE 12 2011
"By the mystery of this water and wine…"

INVENTORY

The (alternate) *Entrance Antiphon* proclaims: "God's love has been poured into our hearts by his Spirit living in us. Alleluia!"[1] What does "pouring" suggest to you? Water poured at Baptism? Wine and water poured together at Mass during the *Presentation of Gifts*? The Holy Spirit poured forth at Pentecost?[2]

INPUT

In the *Opening Prayer* we pray that the Spirit "sent on the Church" will "continue to work in the world through the hearts of all who believe." The *Responsorial* (*Psalm* 104) asks, *"Lord, send out your Spirit and renew the face of the earth."* God does this, first of all, through the *witness* we bear to the Good News by the power of our baptismal consecration as "prophets."

In the *Prayer over the Gifts* we ask as *disciples* that "the Spirit you promised" will "lead us into all truth." And more: "Reveal to us the full meaning of this sacrifice." The Mass is a mystery. We understand it only by the light of the Holy Spirit. The Church calls Eucharist "the source and summit of the Christian life." So in the measure we understand it, we understand the full mystery of the Good News.

We begin to express this mystery explicitly in the *Presentation of Gifts*, when we bring up bread and wine to be transformed into the body and blood of Christ. The presider lifts up the bread, then pours water and wine together into the chalice. This is a symbol of Christ's divinity (the wine) joined to his humanity (the water) at the Incarnation, and of our humanity joined to his divinity by Baptism. As he does he prays: "By the mystery of this water and wine, may we come to share in the divinity of Christ, who humbled himself to share in our humanity."

We already "share in the divinity of Christ" by Baptism. So the intent of the prayer is that we should share *more*, or "more completely" in Christ's divinity. But is "divinity" something quantitative, that we can have more or less of?

We become divine by the "grace" (favor) of sharing in God's divine life. God's life as such cannot be increased or diminished. We can share in it "more" only by *surrendering* ourselves more completely—surrendering our humanity, our human lives, our bodies, minds and wills, our physical activity—to be guided, directed, enlightened and empowered by God's divine life within us. Thinking more and more as God does by surrender to the gift of faith. Desiring more and more what God does by abandonment to the gift of hope. Loving more and more as God does by losing ourselves in union with him through the gift of his divine love. What we are really asking in the prayer is that we might be "poured out," like the water and wine, to be "lost and found" in sharing Christ's divinity, as he was "poured out" to be "lost and found" in sharing our humanity. As Jesus said, "Those who want to save their life will lose it, and those who lose their life for my sake will find it."[3]

In practical terms, the formula for this surrender—for "growing in grace"—is to *let grace express itself in and through our physical words and actions.* We "share more" in the divine life of Christ by letting his life become more *visible* in our actions. This is the definition of Christian *witness*, to which we are committed by our baptismal consecration as *prophets.* And so, when we pray, "By the mystery of [the mingling of] this water and wine, may we come to share [more completely] in the divinity of Christ," we are really praying for continual *conversion*, for the grace to embody more and more visibly in our lifestyle the divine truth and values preached by Jesus and implanted in our hearts by Baptism. In this act we re-affirm our Baptism, and in particular our baptismal consecration as *prophets.*

The *Presentation of Gifts* is a symbolic "re-view" of our Baptism and "pre-view" of the *Eucharistic Prayer.* Baptism made *real* for us the mystery of our dying and rising in Christ. We went down into the water as into the grave, giving up our human lives in order to rise up out of the water a "new creation," the risen body of Christ, living by his divine life. The *Eucharistic Prayer* makes *present* for us the same mystery. The bread and wine become the *real presence* of Christ *offering* himself on the cross, *rising* from the dead and *returning* in triumph and glory: three moments condensed into one in the timeless, eternal "now" of God's experience and made present to us in the mystery of Christ's presence in the Eucharist.

The Eucharist is also the mystery of our presence "in him." We were *in* the body that hung on the cross, because "for our sake God made Jesus *to be sin*" by incorporating us, with all of our sins, into his body on the cross, "so that in him we might become the righteousness of God." In Baptism we "died in him," were "buried with him," "raised with him," and "seated with him in the heavenly places." And when Christ comes in glory at the end of time, he will appear in us, who together will "form that perfect man who is Christ come to full stature." When the host is lifted up at Mass, we are in that host, in the Body that is made present.[4]

In the *Presentation of Gifts*, we "present ourselves" for this, represented by the bread and wine, to be placed on the altar and offered with Christ. Although we sometimes call the *Presentation of Gifts* the "Offertory," it is only a preliminary: the real offering is made during the *Eucharistic Prayer.*

Baptism itself is a preliminary gift of self, one completed by the sacrament of Confirmation. In Baptism we are entirely given. We "die" in Christ and "rise" in him as a "new creation," sharing in the life of God. We "become Christ" as full members of the Church, his body on earth. Still, it is clear in the *Acts of the Apostles* that the Church considers Baptism incomplete without the "Gift of the Spirit," just as the Church was "incomplete" until Pentecost. Jesus "gave birth" to the Church on the cross. In his dying and rising redemption was accomplished. But the Church was not formed or mature enough to be "sent" until the Spirit came.

In this Gift the divine life of Baptism becomes *visible* in our actions. And it is associated with being "sent" as *witnesses* of the Good News. That is what a "witness" is: someone whose visible behavior or style of life raises "irresistible questions" that cannot be answered without the proclamation of the Gospel. That is what it means to be a *prophet*.[5]

In *Acts*, if the Gift of the Spirit was not made manifest at Baptism, it was given later through the "laying on of hands" by an Apostle. We associate this today with the sacrament of Confirmation, in which a bishop, as head of the local church and inheritor of the mission of the Twelve, "confirms" or certifies, that the Church recognizes one's Baptism as "complete," and makes it complete by the "laying on of hands." We were already "saved" as graced members of Christ and of the Church, but now we are officially accepted. And urged to be *mature*.

Grace is life. It *grows* gradually, and reaches maturity in *mission*, just as human life reaches maturity when society judges that one is sufficiently developed to take on adult responsibilities and go to work! This was Paul's point when he urged the Corinthians to "grow up" by making it their focus to "build up the Church."[6]

The first act of "building up the Church" is to bear *witness* to the Good News by letting grace, the life of the risen Jesus within us, become *visible* in our actions. That is witness. For that the Spirit is given. That is what it means to be a "prophet." And to this is we commit ourselves anew in the *Presentation of Gifts*.

[1]See *Romans* 5:5; 8:11.
[2]Poured out as a seal of covenant: *Exodus* 24:6-8; *Leviticus* 4:30; *Matthew* 26:7, 28; *Luke* 22:20. Poured out as self-emptying or offering: *Isaiah* 53:12; *Philippians* 2:7, 17. Poured forth or in as gift: *Isaiah* 44:3; *Ezekiel* 39:29; *Zechariah* 12:10; *Joel* 2:28; *Acts* 2:17, 33; 10:45; *Romans* 5:5; *Titus* 3:6.
[3]See *Philippians* 2:5-11; *Matthew* 10:39; 16:35.
[4]*1Corinthians* 15:18; *2Corinthians* 5:21; *Romans* 6:8; *Ephesians* 1:10; 2:6; 4:7-16; *Colossians* 2:12; 3:1.
[5]*Luke* 24:48-49; *Acts* 1:8; 2:8; 8:14-17; 10:44-47; 19:2-6; Pope Paul VI, *Evangelization in the Modern World*, nos. 21, 42; *The Rites of the Catholic Church*, "Confirmation Within Mass." Homily, no. 22; The Laying on of Hands, nos. 24-25.
[6]*1Corinthnians*, chapters 12-14.

E PLURIBUS UNUM

Acts 2:1-11 tells us that for the Jewish feast of Pentecost—one of the three major festivals: Passover, Pentecost and Tabernacles, that called for a pilgrimage to the holy temple in Jerusalem:[1]—"they were all in one place together." Presumably, this means all the "believers" who *Acts* 1:15 says "numbered about one hundred twenty persons." When the Spirit came, "All of them were filled with the Holy Spirit and began to speak in different tongues, as the Spirit enabled them to proclaim."

At the Tower of Babel pride led to conflicts, violence, and eventual dispersion—which in time led to different languages and inability to communicate. In our day every peer group speaks the special "language of its culture," which both teaches and distorts truth, restricting our ability to understand other people and God himself. God's answer to all this is to pour out his Spirit on the "prophets." These are all the believers who accept their baptismal consecration as prophets and stand up in the power of the "Gift of the Spirit" to challenge the assumptions of their culture, including unexamined teachings and practices of "cultural Catholicism" that the Second Vatican Council "urges all concerned to remove or correct" in the measure that they are abusive, excessive, or defective.[2]

The *Presentation of Gifts* encourages us to trust that, as the bread and wine we bring forward will be transformed into the divine Body and Blood of Christ, we who, like bread, are "fruit of the earth and the work of human hands" can also be transformed and empowered to speak the "language of the Spirit" that reunites the dispersed and divided members of the human race. This is the promise of Eucharist: "Because there is one bread, we who are many are one body, for we all partake of the one bread."[3]

LOSING OURSELVES TO BE FOUND AS ONE

1Corinthians 12:3-13 reminds us that the Spirit unifies:

> There are varieties of gifts, but the same Spirit, varieties of services, but the same Lord, varieties of activities, but the same God who activates all of them in everyone.

The Spirit is given to individuals for the good of the whole community: "To each is given the manifestation of the Spirit for the common good." And so in the *Presentation of Gifts* we

are brought forward as separate hosts, but pledged to be one bread, one Body in Christ.

THROUGH LOCKED DOORS

Prophets can polarize. Those who march by a different drummer can throw those in line out of step. So it is significant that **John 20:19-23** tells us Jesus came through "locked doors." Those who fear the challenge of truth and freedom will divide into clinging groups of partisans—hiding behind locked doors, employing both offensive and defensive tactics for the preservation of their inertia. Jesus sent his Spirit into the Church for deliverance from sin and fear: "Peace.... As the Father has sent me, so I send you.... Whose sins you forgive are forgiven." The prophets say, as Jesus did, "Peace be with you." But there is no true peace, or unity, except in truth and freedom. If the prophets break through locked doors, it is to deliver. *"Lord, send out your Spirit, and renew the face of the earth."*

---

[1]See *Jerome Biblical Commentary*, 1968, on *Exodus* 23:14-17 and J. McKenzie, S.J., *Dictionary of the Bible*: Pentecost was the "day of first fruits" of the grain harvest and became "the anniversary of the giving of the law to Moses"; hence a "renewal of the covenant." For us it is the day of first fruits of the New Covenant, the "birthday of the universal Church."
[2]See Vatican II: *The Church*, nos. 48, 51.
[3]*1Corinthians* 10:17.

INSIGHT
What does the **Presentation of Gifts** *express for you now?*

INITIATIVE
During the **Presentation of Gifts** *recommit to your Baptism and specifically to your baptismal consecration as* **prophet.**

FOR REFLECTION AND DISCUSSION: PENTECOST (Year A)

The Church calls Eucharist "the source and summit of the Christian life." So in the measure we understand it, we understand the full mystery of the Good News. We begin to express this mystery explicitly in the *Presentation of Gifts*, when we bring up bread and wine to be transformed into the body and blood of Christ.

Invitation:

During the *Presentation of Gifts* recommit to your Baptism and specifically to your baptismal consecration as *prophet*.

Ask yourself in prayer and others in discussion: How could the statements below make Mass mean more if we stay aware of them during Mass?

In the *Presentation of Gifts* we are asking that we might be "poured out," like the water and wine, to be "lost and found" in sharing Christ's divinity, as he was "poured out" in his Incarnation to be "lost and found" in our humanity.

We can share "more" in God's life only by *surrendering* ourselves more completely to his divine life within us.

The formula for this surrender is to *let grace express itself in and through our physical words and actions*. This lets his life become more *visible* in our actions, which is the definition of Christian *witness*, to which we are committed as *prophets*.

The Eucharist is also the mystery of our presence "in Christ." We were *in* the body that hung on the cross. We are in the Body made present and lifted up at Mass.

In the "Gift of the Spirit" the divine life of Baptism becomes *visible* in our actions. It is associated with the sacrament of Confirmation and with being "sent" as *witnesses* of the Good News.

The life of grace reaches maturity in *mission*, just as human life reaches maturity when one is sufficiently developed to be able to generate life and to go to work.

The first act of "building up the Church" is to bear *witness* to the Good News by letting grace, the life of the risen Jesus within us, become *visible* in our actions. We commit ourselves to this anew in Confirmation and in the *Presentation of Gifts*.

The *Presentation of Gifts* encourages us to trust that, as the bread and wine will be transformed into the divine Body and Blood of Christ, we can also be transformed and empowered to speak the divine "language of the Spirit" that reunites the dispersed and divided members of the human race.

The Spirit is given to individuals for the good of the whole community. And so in the *Presentation of Gifts* we are brought forward as separate hosts, but pledged to be one bread, one Body in Christ.

Jesus sent his Spirit into the Church for deliverance from sin and fear: "Peace.... As the Father has sent me, so I send you.... Whose sins you forgive are forgiven."

Decisions:

Let the *Presentation of Gifts* remind you of Easter, Baptism, Pentecost, Confirmation.

WHAT HAS THIS BOOKLET DONE FOR YOU?

These reflections were designed to help you deepen your appreciation of the Mass, focusing on the *Presentation of Gifts,* which is the transition from the *Liturgy of the Word* to the *Liturgy of the Eucharist.* This is a moment of *recommitment* to Baptism and Confirmation, and to our sacramental anointing as *prophets.*

By this anointing, we were committed to bear *witness* to Christ as his risen body on earth, and we received the promise of "power from on high"—the Gift of the Holy Spirit. Through significant, conscious, personal recommitment during the *Presentation of Gifts* we enter into the experience of this Gift.

Look back and review what you have seen, asking in particular how you have responded in *choices.* Remember, the effectiveness of input is measured by the authenticity of output.

- How much time did you spend reading and praying over these reflections? Did you come to enjoy this moment in your day?

- Did they motivate you to pay special *attention* to the words and gestures of the *Presentation of Gifts* at Mass?

- What do you know now about sharing in the *mission* of the Church as *prophet* that you didn't know before?

- **More specifically…**

- When the bread and wine are brought forward to be placed on the altar, do you affirm them as representing yourself and symbolically place yourself on the altar with them?

- Do you recognize the words, "which earth has given and human hands have made" as describing yourself, created by God and formed by your choices?

- Do the words, "It will become for us the Bread of life" remind you that Baptism made you divine, a sharer in the divine life of God?

- Does the mingling of the water and wine express to you the mystery of the mingling of the divine and the human in Christ by his Incarnation and in yourself by Baptism?

- Does the pouring of the water and wine increase your desire to be "poured out" to be "lost and found" in Christ's divinity as he was poured out to be lost and found in our humanity?

- When you stand for the prayer, "May the Lord accept the sacrifice at your hands…" are you consciously affirming your participation in this Eucharistic celebration and in the life and mission of the Church?